Telecommunications for Information Specialists

OCLC Library, Information, and Computer Science Series

Telecommunications for Information Specialists

by Larry L. Learn

OCLC Online Computer Library Center, Inc.
6565 Frantz Road
Dublin, Ohio 43017-0702

Printed in the United States of America

ISBN: 1–55653–075–7
       0–933418–35–3 (series)

1   2   3   4   5   I   92   91   90   89

The paper used in this publication meets the minimum requirements of American National Standard for Information Science—Permanence of Paper for Printed Library Material, ANSI Z39.48-1984.   ∞™

Library of Congress Cataloging-in-Publication Data

Learn, Larry L., 1943–
   Telecommunications for information specialists.

   (OCLC library, information, and computer science series ; 11)
   Bibliography: p.
   Includes index.
   1. Telecommunication in libraries. 2. Libraries—Communication systems. 3. Information services—Communication systems. 4. Library information networks. 5. Information technology.
I. Title. II. Series.
Z680.5.L43 1989 021.6'5   89-8601
ISBN 1–55653–075–7
ISBN 0–933418–35–3 (series)

*"I hold that man is in the right who is
most closely in league with the future."*
Henrik Ibsen [1828–1906]

Contents

"All our knowledge has its origins in our perceptions."
Leonardo da Vinci [1452–1519]

Figures

Tables

*"Around the Earth Thoughts Shall Fly
In the Twinkling of an Eye."*
Ursula Sonthiel (Mother Shipton) [1488–1561]

Preface

Telecommunications has evolved to play a major role in library and information science, a role that continues to become more important with each passing day. As we move into the "electronic information age," it is critical that information science professionals have a sound understanding of this often complex and sometimes difficult area.

Unlike some other fields, it is impossible to write a definitive book on the topic; it would be out of date soon after the manuscript was written due to the volatile and dynamic state of the current telecommunications environment. Further, the current literature within the telecommunications arena is typically geared toward telecommunications professionals and is often difficult, if not impossible, to put into perspective without a good understanding of the complex and often counter-intuitive nature of the field.

Audience

As the title implies, this book is targeted toward information specialists. It assumes little, if any, prior knowledge of the field, and is designed to be an encompassing overview, rather than a "how-to" book. It is anticipated that the reader, after having completed the book, will be prepared to survey and comprehend most of the general current literature in the field and understand and interpret the impact of major developments. An extensive glossary of telecommunications acronyms and terms assists the reader. A comprehensive bibliography is also included, to acknowledge the work of others upon which the author has drawn and to provide sources for further exploration.

A unique feature of this book is its study guide. Professors of library and information science who are looking for a practical introductory text for this complicated topic will find that this guide, used in conjunction with the glossary and bibliography, makes the book a valuable classroom resource. Practicing professionals interested in further examining their understanding of the material presented will also find the study guide to be useful.

The intent of this book is to provide the fundamental background that is needed to enable the reader to better follow current developments, to better assess the potential impact of these developments on individual situations, and to better plan for the future.

Acknowledgments

The author gratefully acknowledges C. Edward Wall, publisher of the Pierian Press family of publications, which includes *Library Hi Tech Journal* and *Library Hi Tech News,* for his encouragement and cooperation with this project. The content of some of the material in this book originally appeared in the Pierian publications, but has been updated and augmented for this book. The author is also deeply indebted to his colleagues at OCLC for their cooperation, advice, and assistance with the publication. Many have helped, but Sig Dierk, Rick Limes, Becky Wright, and Lois Yoakam deserve special thanks.

Last, but not least, as is reflected in the bibliography, the author has drawn heavily on the efforts of others, to whom he is deeply indebted.

*"There is nothing more difficult to take in hand, more perilous
to conduct, or more uncertain in its success, than to take
the lead in the introduction of a new order of things."
(The Prince) Niccolo Machiavelli [1469–1527]*

Introduction

Telecommunications, to a greater extent than most other information science related areas, has recently undergone significant and rapid change with diverse and complex implications for libraries, information services and information systems design. The impetus for this change has come from the political, legislative, regulatory and judicial processes, as well as significant and rapid technological advances. Changing roles, economic factors and industry trends, as well as changing user capabilities, expectations, and demands have further exacerbated the situation. The current telecommunications environment has significant implications for most organizations — particularly information related organizations — in terms of not only present, but more importantly, future operations. In many organizations, decisions crucial to future success or failure are being made in the telecommunications area, or areas critically impacted by telecommunications, in response to the changing environment. To be optimal, these decisions must not only be conditioned by a general understanding of the current telecommunications environment, but also by what the future is likely to bring.

Technical innovation in telecommunications can best be described as being in its infancy. Technologies such as optical fibers, satellites, and microwave and cellular radio have the potential for allowing "bypass" of the traditional telecommunications system. Recent developments in the field of photonics and developments such as ballistic transistors point to continued and significant evolution within the field. Technological innovation is also occurring at the implementation level. Statistical multiplexors, line extenders, smart modems, and a vast array of "smart" communication devices are available to help maximize the efficiency and effectiveness of the telecommunications environment. The power and ready availability of relatively inexpensive microprocessor technology have resulted in a dramatic shift in the distribution of processor power, portending major change in the characteristics of many information networks.

Telecommunications within future library and information systems can no longer be viewed as simply a means of connecting terminals to computers, but in the final analysis should be viewed as an information delivery system that makes information, in many forms and formats, available quickly, easily, and economically to (and between) a wide variety of users through an array of access mechanisms including computers and storage devices, intelligent workstations, document delivery stations, microprocessors, and local area networks.

Telecommunications networks have come to play an ever increasing and vital role in libraries and the organizations and institutions they serve, and this trend is continuing at an accelerated pace. Beyond the scope of the local institution, statewide, multistate, nationwide, and even international networks have evolved or are evolving to play an even more important role in the services libraries perform, and the way libraries provide these services. Yet many have found it difficult to keep abreast of developments in this area, and understandably so. The technology is complex and changing at a dizzying pace, and the telecommunications industry structure is undergoing revolutionary change in the wake of the breakup of the Bell System and the substantial and ongoing restructuring of the related legal and regulatory environment. Further, the telecommunications networks themselves have fostered new relationships and opportunities as libraries expand their institutional and geographic scope.

Much of the current library and information systems literature focuses on application of networks, yet it is equally important for the practicing professional to have a current working knowledge of the telecommunications infrastructure upon which these applications are built. This is particularly true since the telecommunications infrastructure is extremely dynamic, and the effectiveness of many network applications will be determined by the form this infrastructure takes in the future. To be optimum, future applications must be targeted toward the environment in which they will exist and operate. At a minimum, they must be able to compensate for change in the environment. This is further accentuated by the magnitude of investment required by many of these endeavors.

This book, with its glossary, bibliography, and study guide, is designed to provide the library and information system professional with the broad understanding of the issues and elements of the evolving field of telecommunications that will be essential to sound decision making in the areas of library and information system automation, and most importantly the emerging area of online information and document delivery. The field of telecommunications has historically been a mostly unique discipline, and as such, it is often difficult for professionals in other areas to assimilate current information and developments and to put this new information into an overall framework. This is particularly true since the field is a unique mixture of regulation and technology, which sometimes leads to counter-intuitive results and practices. The knowledge platform developed within the book, apart from its own usefulness, is designed to serve as a "launching pad" for ongoing reading and learning within this very dynamic and rapidly changing field.

2

The Role of Telecommunications

To better conceptualize the role of telecommunications and its relationship to other elements of automated information systems, it may be useful to consider the following paradigm:

A telecommunications network is like a shipping business.

Within a shipping operation there are three basic elements:

1. The freight that must be transported

2. The highways and surface roads upon which the trucks travel

3. The truck, or other vehicle (for this discussion, we will consider a trucking operation), that is employed to do the actual transport

Comparing this model with an automated information system, the freight represents the need (i.e., capability, functionality, etc.) that is to be addressed by the system, the truck represents the computer application program or implementation that addresses the identified need, and the highway is the telecommunications infrastructure that carries the information associated with the application program.

The Freight

The needs that a system must satisfy are generally somewhat inflexible. They are determined (or at least should be) by the users of the system, and should be responsive to the users' environment. Although there may be some flexibility to accommodate the other elements of the system, this is often rather limited. For example, when the freight is a liquid, it may be possible to design the tank that contains it to be long and cylindrical in form, rather than spherical (which would provide the highest ratio of volume to surface and thus the most economical containment), realizing that this concession will better accommodate the need to traverse a highway, pass under bridges, and not exceed the width restrictions

3

imposed by the highway structure, while still containing the required volume of liquid.

It must also be recognized that the design, development, and implementation of the completed system will likely take some period of time, and as the freight is packaged, it should be packaged where possible with a realization of the parameters of the system that will exist at the time the freight is actually shipped, rather than considering only the current environmental parameters.

The Highways

At the other end of the model, the telecommunications infrastructure (highway) is mostly determined by factors external to the system. This infrastructure, like an interstate highway system, represents a solution to the needs of many sectors within the broader spectrum of communications users. Being very expensive to build and maintain, the national/international telecommunications infrastructure can only be realized if it accommodates the needs of a broad spectrum of users. Furthermore, this infrastructure is very dynamic, changing rapidly and substantively with time. Therefore, from the perspective of the information system designer, the telecommunications infrastructure represents a changing, but relatively inflexible boundary which any system must accommodate to be effective.

The Truck

The application program or implementation (truck) is where the rubber meets the road. This must be a critical area of accommodation and flexibility. Typically caught between relatively inflexible users' needs and an inflexible telecommunications infrastructure, the application must match these needs with the infrastructure. Further, since both the needs and the infrastructure are changing with time, the application must focus on an implementation time line. That is, it must match changing needs at given points in time with a changing infrastructure at the same points in time, and must do this with a certain degree of flexibility to minimize the risk that the specific implementation, at a given point in time, will not accommodate this critical match.

The Approach

It is clear that to design and implement an effective information system, where telecommunications will be involved, it is necessary to have a good understanding of the users' needs, the system technology, and the telecommunications infrastructure, and that this understanding must not only be based on the current environment, but also on the future evolution of these elements. It is not the intention of this book to address either users' needs, or to any significant extent, automated systems technology, but rather to address the third area, the telecommunications infrastructure — the highways of the automated information system domain.

Implications

Many implications can be drawn from this model and approach. The system designer — or the library or information system professional looking to acquire such a system — must make a valiant effort to understand the evolving telecommunications infrastructure; the highway system upon which the application must, by necessity, run. If the trucks are too high, too wide, too long, or too heavy, there will be serious problems. Further, the trucks must be designed to accommodate the intended freight. It would make little sense to build flat-bed trucks to transport fuel oil. Efficiency results where the freight is packaged to best meet the needs of the shipping mechanism. Where flexibility in packaging the freight exists, this should be used to better accommodate the potential constraints or opportunities offered by the shipping mechanism.

It must also be realized that the system is often dynamic and evolutionary, and that change may bring discontinuity. Such discontinuity (e.g., the need to upgrade hardware, change transmission mechanisms or services, etc.) must be planned for wherever possible. Another opportunity too often lost, is the opportunity to focus risks within a system where they can most easily be accommodated.

Summary

Like a commercial shipping operation, an automated information system requires the best balance of:

1. *Capability:* In the final analysis, the system must haul the freight efficiently and effectively.

2. *Quality of Service:* The freight must get to its final destination safely and within an acceptable time frame.

3. *Cost:* The shipper must attain the *best* price for accomplishing items 1 and 2. Unfortunately, too often cost is considered first rather than last in this regard, with significant detrimental effects.

The focus of subsequent chapters within this book is an attempt to help the library and information system professional better understand the evolving telecommunications infrastructure, including the regulatory, industry, and technological aspects, that they might have a better "grip on the road" — what it looks like now, and where it will likely go in the future — as they plan for automation and the delivery of services using telecommunications.

3

"Legislation, like fine sausage, is best not viewed in the making."
Otto von Bismarck [1815–1898]

Regulation

Any discussion of the telecommunications environment would not be complete without the recognition that government regulation is inextricably interwoven into the fabric of the field. The industry has been regulated for more than 50 years. The Communications Act of 1934 established the federal regulatory machinery and the concept of universal service as a national telecommunications policy. Easy and affordable access to a universal telecommunications system was considered to be in the national interest. The result has been a large regulated monopoly where universal service was achieved by subsidizing costly access, particularly in more remote areas, with revenues from more lucrative services (e.g., long-distance service).

In recent years the goal of universal access has been substantially achieved, and beginning around 1956 the federal government pursued a policy toward progressive deregulation designed to foster competition within the telecommunications industry. Prior to 1956, a relatively recent date, the Bell System enjoyed nearly total dominance over the whole of the telecommunications infrastructure within the United States. The most significant event to affect the telecommunications environment in more recent history was the break-up of the monolithic Bell system. This was however, only one among many important factors which have affected telecommunications in the past and will continue to do so in the future.

Recent Regulatory and Judicial Milestones

In 1956, a non-Bell phone attachment was allowed for the first time. The so-called HUSH-A-PHONE was a cup attached to the telephone handset to allow conversation to be muffled. Prior to this, Bell had been able to prevent any "foreign" attachments from being used with its equipment. In 1959, private organizations were allowed microwave communications in a spectrum above 890 MHz. Previously, this spectrum was available only to AT&T. In 1968, the Federal Communications

Commission (FCC) for the first time allowed a foreign device, called a Carterfone, to be directly connected to the Bell network. The Carterfone was a two-way radio device which connected to and used the Bell network, allowing radio-to-phone communications. This decision gave rise to the so-called interconnect industry, allowing privately owned branch exchange (PBX) and key telephone systems to be connected to the telephone network as long as a protective "interface coupler" was installed between the private equipment and the Bell network.

MCI Communications Corporation was allowed to install and operate a microwave communications system between Chicago and St. Louis in 1969, leading to a private-line service offering to business customers. This was the first time a private company (other than AT&T) had attempted to engage in a business solely designed to resell long-distance services to other organizations. In 1971, the FCC authorized MCI-type organizations to operate on a nationwide basis. These so-called specialized common carriers (SCCs) were allowed to use Bell local lines to connect customers to its private long-distance transmission equipment.

In 1972, the FCC extended the 1959 microwave ruling to encourage competition in the emerging satellite communications industry, and not until 1977 did the FCC allow the SCCs to provide nondedicated, dial-up, long-distance services to their customers. It wasn't until 1981 that the FCC allowed unregulated, nondominant (i.e., other than AT&T) organizations the ability to share and resell interstate long-distance service to others. Consequently, private organizations could buy bulk-rate transmission lines and resell these services to others at a profit.

As evidenced by the above, AT&T has had until very recently nearly complete dominance over interstate transmission of signals and, as such, controlled the market for long-distance communication. In addition to the above FCC actions, several judicial actions have played an important role in the evolution of the telecommunications industry.

1949 Antitrust Action

In 1949, the U.S. Justice Department filed an antitrust suit seeking to separate Western Electric from AT&T. The suit was eventually resolved in 1956, when the Bell System agreed to restrict itself to common carrier communications and license its technology to competitors. Hence, it was prohibited from participating in the data processing or information processing arena. As time passed and telecommunications and computer technology began to merge, this prohibition grew increasingly intolerable for the Bell System.

Computer Inquiry I

Consequently, in 1966 the FCC launched a five-year inquiry, now known as Computer Inquiry I (CI-I), into the relationship between telecommunications and computers. In 1971, the FCC ruled that (with minor exceptions) common carriers could provide data processing services to entities other than themselves through completely separate affiliates. These so-called structural separations were instituted to minimize the ability of the carriers to engage in cross-subsidization between regulated communications and unregulated computer services.

Computer Inquiry II

By 1976, the convergence of computer and communications technologies had progressed to the point where it was difficult, if not impossible, to clearly delineate data communications from data processing services, and the FCC launched a second inquiry, Computer Inquiry II (CI-II), into the matter. Four years later, the FCC ruled that it would no longer attempt to define data processing separately from data communications, and established two new classes of services: basic and enhanced. Basic services were, in essence, services that carried information unchanged through the network from source to destination, while enhanced services were anything beyond basic services. Effective January 1, 1982, enhanced services were no longer subjected to FCC regulation. Regulated carriers were then free to offer enhanced services, but only through separate subsidiaries (i.e., the service distinctions changed, while the structural separations requirements remained as before). The CI-II decision effectively allowed AT&T to enter fields previously prohibited by the 1956 consent decree.

1974 Antitrust Action (Divestiture)

In 1974 the Justice Department again brought an antitrust action against AT&T, seeking to dismantle the Bell System. In January of 1982, AT&T signed a consent decree agreeing to divest itself of the local portions of its 22 local operating companies (BOCs). This has come to be known as the much publicized "Divestiture" agreement. On January 1, 1984, Divestiture effectively separated universal access, which was supported primarily by the local telephone company, from the long-distance services provided by AT&T — services which had historically subsidized local access. The legal separation of AT&T from the local companies required new tariffs with a new structure.

Post-Divestiture Industry Structure

The FCC moved all of the telecommunications industry in the direction of a cost-based rate structure with its 1983 access-charge decision [*MTS and WATS Market Structure, Phase I*, Third Report and Order, 93 FCC 2d 241, 1983]. This allowed local telephone companies to recover lost subsidization by assessing the local subscribers. Thus, a local telephone user would have to pay for the privilege of being connected to the complete (i.e., long-distance) telecommunications network. The decision also provided for recovery of legitimate local costs in support of long-distance service by prescribing circuit termination charges to be assessed on long-distance carriers and other private networks which make use of the local facilities. Thus the long-distance services would pay a surcharge for connecting to a local telephone.

On October 3, 1983, AT&T filed new tariffs with the FCC which reflected a cost-based structure and were designed to take into account the separation of the local companies. The new structure placed a significantly increased financial burden on users with a substantial need for local access (e.g., library and information systems like the OCLC Online System). This shift in financial burden was not met with enthusiastic and widespread approval. Pressure was brought on Congress to mandate low local-subscriber rates. Under pressure from Congress the FCC delayed implementation of the new tariffs, which were subsequently withdrawn by AT&T.

The tariffs would have increased the telecommunications costs of library and information systems substantially. The average impact upon OCLC, for example, initially would have been an increase in the neighborhood of 70%. Even after OCLC (among others) asked the FCC for a waiver of a $25 per terminal access surcharge for "leaking" long-distance telephone calls onto the local telephone network from private lines (i.e., something technically impossible from the OCLC Online System at that time), and the FCC agreed, the overall impact still remained in the neighborhood of 55% (although the waiver reduced the OCLC increase by nearly $1 million per year).

In addition to the AT&T tariffs, the National Exchange Carriers Association (NECA) also files tariffs reflecting the rates their local telephone companies (local exchange carriers or LECs) assess customers (including AT&T) for use of the local telephone network. As a result of Divestiture, NECA filed the required tariffs, which were subsequently found — after much controversy — by the FCC to be unlawful. In December of 1984, NECA again filed new tariffs with the FCC, which subsequently became effective on April 1, 1985. In apparent response to the NECA tariffs, AT&T filed new tariffs in January of 1985. The AT&T tariffs again reflected significant increases for library and information services. For example, the impact on OCLC was in the neighborhood of 30% overall (but varied widely from about 10% to 70%, depending upon specific location). Through the intervention of OCLC and others, the effects were eventually reduced to around 20%. The AT&T tariffs became effective on April 27, 1985.

It should be noted that under the restructured tariffs, long-distance rates have actually decreased while local-access rates have significantly increased in most areas. This has provided an economic incentive for large businesses, or other organizations, to bypass the local telephone network and access the long-distance facilities directly. In some instances these organizations also bypass the long-distance carriers (i.e., end-to-end) using satellite facilities, private fiber-optic or microwave systems, etc. The impact of such bypass is to erode the base of support for the local telephone network and subsequently force an increase in the burden of support for the local telephone network to be borne by those subscribers who have not (or cannot) bypass the local network. The topic of bypass is discussed later in more detail.

Computer Inquiry III

As the market for enhanced services (e.g., valued-added networks, or VANs, electronic mail services, database services, etc.) evolved, and more enhanced service providers (ESPs) came into existence, it became clear that the type, availability, and cost of basic services were critical to these ESPs — particularly where competition involved affiliates of the regulated carriers. In 1986, the FCC launched its Computer Inquiry III (CI-III), in which the FCC proposed to substitute nonstructural safeguards for existing CI-II subsidiary rules.

Open Network Architecture (ONA)

In place of structural safeguards, the FCC imposed new rules requiring AT&T and the Bell operating companies (BOCs) to offer enhanced services based on a new Open Network Architecture (ONA) model, and further required them to submit ONA plans by February 1, 1988. This meant these companies must offer the basic services supporting enhanced services on an unbundled basis to all ESPs under the same terms and conditions as to their own operations. The companies were allowed to offer specific enhanced services prior to the 1988 deadline, provided their plans to handle comparably efficient interconnection (CEI) — the name given to the specific case-by-case application of the more general ONA — and various other accounting and reporting requirements met with FCC approval (i.e., CEI needed specific case-by-case approval, while once ONA was in place, the various services would be available to all). It should be noted that under terms of Divestiture, AT&T (prior to 1991) and the BOCs were prohibited from providing information services, which are an important and potentially lucrative subset of enhanced services, although the prohibition can be waived by the court on a case-by-case basis; something that has recently taken place to a limited extent.

The ONA model provides for "basic service elements" (BSEs) that will be made available to ESPs on an unbundled basis, and "basic serving arrangements" (BSAs) that will be used by the ESPs to gain access to the BSEs. The BOCs will provide both BSEs and BSAs, although some BOCs are proposing that the ESPs use currently tariffed special-access, or so-called private-line, circuits to gain access to the BSEs. AT&T, on the other hand, will provide nondiscriminatory interLATA transport of the BOCs' BSEs. There has been considerable controversy surrounding the definition, tariffing, scheduling, and pricing of the various BSEs and BSAs, and as the manuscript for this book is being completed, the ONA issue is still very much unresolved.

Rate-of-Return Regulation

The regulated telephone companies have historically been subject to rate-of-return regulation. Under the rate-of-return regulatory regime, prices for regulated services flow from the carriers' revenue requirements as determined by the regulatory process. In simple terms, the process begins by determining the type of services that will be offered, including estimates of the volume of usage for each service. From these estimates, the carrier's investment in plant and equipment (so-called rate base), and various operations costs are determined. In general terms, the regulated revenue requirement is then determined to be the operations costs, which are not included in the rate base, plus the carrier's regulated rate-of-return (typically about 12%) multiplied by the rate base. The regulated price for a specific service results from simply dividing the specific regulatory revenue requirement by the forecast volume of demand for that service to arrive at a per-unit price.

Since the carrier's profit under rate-of-return regulation is determined by the size of the rate base and the allowed regulated rate-of-return, perverse incentives exist for the carrier to maximize investment in the rate base, often called gold plating, while placing less emphasis on operations costs which simply fall directly into the regulated revenue requirement and are included in the price. Depreciation of the rate base is treated as an operations cost, and also falls directly into the price.

Price Cap Regulation

On August 21, 1987, the FCC issued a Notice of Proposed Rulemaking [Docket 87-313] proposing to put a cap on phone prices, rather than limit the profits of the phone companies, as is the case under rate-of-return regulation. Although the initial proposal didn't make much headway, it sparked an explosion of controversy. A major criticism was the lack of specifics contained in the proposal. On May 12, 1988, the FCC voted to offer for public comment a highly detailed price-cap proposal that would allow AT&T and many local exchange carriers (LECs) to voluntarily use price caps instead of the current rate-of-return regulation. If adopted, the plan would take effect April 1, 1989, and would be based on the prices then in effect.

The price-cap proposal would place an upper limit on aggregate prices that would consist of four elements:

1. The current price for existing services would serve as the starting point for the cap price.

2. An inflation factor based on the Gross National Product Price Index would subsequently be applied.

3. A productivity factor intended to reflect productivity gains anticipated within the telecommunications industry would be applied.

4. A noncontrollable cost factor designed to further reflect upward or downward changes in costs that the carriers cannot control (e.g., taxes) would be applied.

Under the proposal, a carrier's profits would no longer be regulated, and any additional profits brought about by increases in efficiency, cost containment, etc., would flow directly to the carrier.

Unlike the current rate-of-return regulatory mechanism, the price-cap proposal does not fix prices for specific services, but rather places the various services in "baskets," capping prices for the aggregate of services in each of four baskets. AT&T services would be divided between two baskets: switched services (e.g., long-distance phone service); and private-line services. Local carriers would also see their services divided between two baskets: switched access services and all other interstate services, which consist primarily of special access or private-line services. Therefore, in the general sense of the phrase, specific service prices are not actually capped. For example, it would be possible to lower prices for certain private-line services used only by very large customers, while raising prices on other private-line services that are used by libraries and library database providers. Although this might not change the aggregate price of the services within the private-line basket, it would certainly reflect price increases for the libraries and library database providers. The price-cap proposal remains embroiled in controversy without a resolution as the manuscript for this book is being completed.

Divestiture

The breakup of the Bell System resulted in the separation of the 22 local Bell operating companies (BOCs) from the parent AT&T. This not only resulted in major structural changes for the Bell System, but also significantly changed the way customers interact with, and are serviced by the carriers.

The Bell System is now separated into AT&T and seven regional holding companies (RHCs), each consisting of several of the original 22 BOCs. The BOCs have authority to provide local telephone service within defined geographic regions called Local Access and Transport Areas (LATAs). AT&T and other interexchange carriers (e.g., MCI) provide long-distance service between LATAs. InterLATA service that is interstate in nature is provided under the jurisdiction of the FCC. If the interLATA service is contained within a state, the respective state regulatory authority has jurisdiction.

The most apparent impact of Divestiture on the typical user is the resulting complication of multiple vendors involved in ordering and delivering telecommunications services. First, there is the local-access line provided by the local telephone company. Second, the user must obtain a telephone instrument, etc., from a separate vendor or a subsidiary of AT&T or the telephone company. Third, long-distance service must be obtained from yet another vendor (e.g., AT&T, MCI, etc.). In the case of end-to-end service, the local telephone company on the far end of the circuit must also be contacted (although the option to obtain end-to-end service from the interexchange carrier exists — for a price).

Another impact has been the complexity of administration. The typical home telephone bill was a relatively simple document, usually no more than one or two pages, before Divestiture. After Divestiture, the document contained itemized lists of local service, and possibly long-distance calls carried by the local telephone company. Long-distance calls are itemized separately by AT&T or other interexchange carriers that may also send entirely separate bills to the customer. Additionally, leased telephone equipment (or equipment purchased during the billing period) is also itemized. Large organizations have been affected even more severely (e.g., the OCLC monthly telephone bill increased from around 400 pages to 3,300 pages). The additional administrative complexity also increased the time required to process orders and install or change service (e.g., OCLC telecommunications activities were severely affected for nearly a year).

FCC Certification of Computer Equipment

Computers and similar electronic equipment that use digital techniques generate and use radio frequency (RF) energy for timing and control purposes. Unless precautions are taken, this energy can escape from these devices and cause interference with other equipment — often television, radio, medical, or telecommunications systems. For this reason, manufacturers are required by the Federal Communications Commission (FCC) to meet certain requirements and to submit their equipment for testing and certification.

The FCC allows two classes of certification for computer equipment. Class A, the less restrictive of the two classes, is intended for equipment that will *not* be operated in residential environments, while Class B, the more restrictive class, is intended to include operation of the equipment in residential environments. The distinction between residential and commercial environments is felt to be needed for at least two reasons:

1. Residential environments tend to have more equipment (e.g., television sets, radios, high-fidelity audio systems, etc., operated both by the computer consumer and neighbors!) with which the computer equipment can interfere.

2. Since the onus is on the equipment operator to correct interference or cease operation, the Commission felt that commercial operators needed less protection than residential consumers.

Knowledge of computer device certification is important for several reasons. First, it is important that these devices be installed and operated according to the manufacturers' instructions, and that any equipment, cables, etc., that might be used in conjunction with the equipment also be certified for such use. Second, it is important that users ensure that equipment that they buy has met these FCC certification requirements, since noncompliance among various equipment manufacturers is not uncommon, and the financial and technical responsibility for correcting any resulting problems rests with the consumer. Last, at least in the case of computer equipment certification, a "B" is better than an "A." It is important that the consumer of this equipment recognize the distinction, and acquire the proper Class of equipment for the intended application. It should also be noted that FCC certification only indicates the equipment meets RF radiation standards, not that the equipment functions as intended or expected.

Although not directly related to computer-device certification, it should also be noted that the FCC requires certification of all equipment that is attached to the public telephone network. Therefore, it is important that the user ascertain that any device that is procured with the intent of attaching it to the public network (i.e., telephone instruments, modems, multiplexors, etc.) have the necessary FCC certifications. Again, such certification indicates only that the equipment meets FCC specifications designed to prevent damage to the public network, and has little, if any, bearing on how well the equipment might otherwise function. It should also be noted that the FCC requires that telephone instruments located in public areas, or intended for use in emergency situations, be hearing-aid compatible.

Inside Wiring

Undoubtedly, the simplest element of telecommunications technology is the copper wire that still carries most of the signals at and near the user site. After all, this is the same technology that was introduced with the advent of the first telegraph machine. Spotlighting the propensity for the telecommunications industry to make even the very simple extraordinarily complex, this so-called premises or inside wiring has become one of the more complex, confusing and problematic elements of many telecommunications installations.

The problem most often presents itself to libraries in one of two contexts. The first is associated with the installation and maintenance of special access, or so-called private-line circuits most commonly used in libraries to provide access to remote computer services. The second is associated with the installation and maintenance of telephones and related equipment, particularly in campus settings.

To better understand the problem, it may be helpful to examine the distinctions among:

1. Ownership of the wire

2. Provision of installation and/or maintenance services by a regulated carrier under tariff

3. Regulation of installation and/or maintenance services, as these relate to the wire

In particular, installation and/or maintenance services may be regulated, regardless of who happens to own the respective wire, or whether or not the services are provided under tariff. In fact, many inside-wire installation and maintenance services have historically been performed by local exchange carriers (LECs) on a regulated, but untariffed basis. Deregulating these services often means that the LEC is simply required to account for the revenues and costs related to these services separately from its regulated operations. Provision of these services under tariff results in the detailed specification of rates, terms and conditions under which the services *must* be provided, and more importantly, specifically limits the provision of the services to the circumstances and the manner described in the tariff.

Deregulation of Inside Wire

In 1980, the FCC deregulated so-called customer premises equipment (CPE), such as telephone instruments, telephone answering machines, and PBXs. Related to that decision, in 1981 the FCC deregulated installation of new "complex" cable [FCC CC Docket 79-105]. Complex cable, including associated components and necessary conduit, connects telecommunications equipment shared by multiple users with telephones, terminals, and other related equipment usually located within the same building or in buildings on contiguous property, as is often the case in college and university campus environments. Providers, other than the telephone company, were then free to install this wire subject to the constraint that it must meet the technical specifications set forth by the FCC [47 **CFR**, Part 68] before the system could be attached to the public telephone network.

So-called simple wire, installed in residences and small businesses with one or two telephone lines, was not included in the 1981 FCC ruling. Deregulation of installation and maintenance of simple wire, as well as maintenance of complex wire was ordered by the FCC in January of 1987 (except in New York, where the effective date is 1990). The deregulation of these services neither prohibited the LEC from offering the services nor required that the LECs offer the services through separate subsidiaries. In fact, it allowed the LECs the option of not offering the services at all. They were, however, prohibited from imposing any maintenance or use charges on deregulated cable. The LECs were allowed to collect inside wiring maintenance fees on an untariffed basis from anyone who *chose* to use that service, provided the LECs accounted for the activity in the appropriate accounts designated for unregulated activities. In certain instances, the user was then confronted with the problem of arranging for the installation of the last few feet of wire between the end of the LEC-provided circuit and the user's telephone or modem. This also gave rise, in some telephone companies, to the questionable practice of placing an inside wiring maintenance fee on a user's monthly bill with a note stating that by not contacting the LEC and asking that the service not be rendered, the user was agreeing to subscribe to the service, thus some users are paying for an optional service to which they may not wish to subscribe.

Ownership of Inside Wire

The issue of ownership of inside wire was made even more confusing. Initially, the FCC ordered the LECs to relinquish ownership of most of the inside wire that they had either previously expensed or fully amortized (i.e., that had been completely charged to the ratepayer). At the same time, the FCC decided not to attempt to determine ownership of the wiring once it had been relinquished by the LEC, but left this issue to be resolved through the application of local property law. In other words, under certain circumstances, particularly when the local subscriber was not the building or property owner, it was clear that the LEC did not own the wire, but not at all clear who actually did own the wire, and hence, who was responsible for maintenance and repair.

Grey and Black Cable

The issue was further complicated by the fact that the FCC order only affected inside wire that the LEC had charged to account number 232 of the federally mandated accounting schedule. All inside wire had not been charged to this account. Rather, inside wire that was used to go between building floors (so-called riser cable) or between telephone distribution "closets" (so-called distribution cable) had been charged to account 242 and was not addressed in the FCC order — a source of much confusion. Although the deregulated (so-called 232, or grey) cable typically had a grey-color covering, while the regulated (so-called 242, or black) cable typically had a black-color covering, this was not always the case (e.g., so-called grey cable that was actually black, and black cable that was actually grey). The common use of the terminology grey and black cable has, unfortunately, led to even more confusion. In addition, the FCC ordered the LECs to fully amortize and relinquish ownership of all 232 cable by 1994.

Reviewing the Situation

Before introducing any more complexity, it might be helpful to summarize the ownership situation, as it then existed. Putting aside the issue of black wire, which the FCC did not initially address, there were basically three kinds of wire:

1. Inside wire that had been installed by the user or his contractor subsequent to deregulation of this function, which was owned by the user

2. Inside wire that the LEC had either expensed or fully amortized, which was clearly not owned by the LEC, but in certain instances the ownership of which was not clear.

3. Inside wire in which the LEC retained a capital interest, which was owned by the LEC until the investment was fully amortized, but in no instance later than 1994.

Further, it was the "owner's" responsibility to maintain his own wire.

Although in principle this seems straightforward, it must be realized that in most instances the inside wire had been installed at different times in the same conduits, with little or no effort having been expended to identify the specific wires. Hence, when a problem arose, it could be a monumental undertaking simply identifying which wire it was, and hence whose responsibility it would be to fix it — particularly where some of the wire installed by the LEC had been fully amortized (i.e., no longer owned by the LEC) and some remained to be fully amortized.

State and Federal Issues

Since the inside wire is also typically used to carry intrastate communications, state regulators generally had established amortization schedules for the LECs for that portion of the wiring investment attributed to intrastate use. In many instances, the state amortization schedules were longer than those established by the FCC, which resulted in lower local telephone rates. To enforce its order it was necessary for the FCC to invoke federal supremacy, or "preemption" of state jurisdictional authority — something not well received by the state regulators, and which subsequently resulted in appeals and court challenges.

In the wake of the state challenges and a U.S. Supreme Court decision [*Louisiana v. the FCC*, 1986] that appeared to place certain limits on the FCC's authority to preempt state regulation, particularly in the area of amortization of intrastate telecommunications equipment, the FCC subsequently eliminated the requirement that the LECs relinquish ownership of inside wiring. This not only eased some of the confusion over inside-wire ownership, but also avoided a confrontation with state regulators over the issue of conflicting amortization schedules. This did little, however, to aid users in distinguishing between wire installed by the user from wire installed and owned by the LEC, or wire installed by the LEC, but subsequently purchased by the user — a critical issue with regard to establishing maintenance responsibility for a specific wire.

Network Boundaries

Since the black wire remained regulated, spare capacity that might exist in this cable could not be used by the customer, for example, to connect terminals to local computers. The FCC has subsequently ruled that under certain conditions the subscriber or building owner can request that the public network demarcation point, or so-called network interface (NI), or point of connection to the public network, be moved to the building cable entrance or some other convenient location. After reimbursing the LEC for the black cable, the customer has access to this cable. In a further attempt to simplify the black wire situation, the FCC allowed the LECs to transfer their investment in this cable to the 232 account, where it can be amortized in a manner similar to complex cable. This, however, can be done either on a systemwide basis, or on a case-by-case basis, thus retaining much of the troublesome complexity.

The FCC has also defined the network interface (NI) in functional rather than physical terms. The NI is the point where the LEC's regulated responsibility ends and nonregulated customer responsibility begins. Unfortunately, exactly where the NI is located may depend, among other factors, on state regulatory body preferences, the specific telecommunications service involved, the age of the building, or the number of tenants in the building. Since the various LECs have significant leeway for variation in actual practices, this has created substantial problems and confusion, not only where different companies are involved, but also within a given company on a state-by-state, or case-by-case basis.

Most, but certainly not all, LECs have now adopted a "minimum point of termination" (MPOT) policy, where they run their regulated service to the closest point necessary to bring the service to the customer or building owner. Sometimes, however, the NI is brought to the user's floor or nearest telephone closet, and sometimes all the way to the user's desk. Some companies have also chosen to follow different policies for different services. This can become a particularly troublesome issue where multi-building business complexes, or college or university campuses are involved. Keeping track and dealing with these diverse practices can also be a significant staff and overhead expense for large networks (e.g., the OCLC network) that acquire services directly or indirectly from some 1,400 or more LECs throughout the various states. For example, some LECs will only run entrance cable to an MPOT in one building in a multi-building complex, while others will run cable to an MPOT in each building.

Campus Wiring Systems

In addition, many colleges and universities, as well as business complexes and high-rise office buildings, are now installing total building or campus wiring systems. This can cause a problem in situations where the LEC has to extend its service beyond its MPOT. As an example, private lines, such as those used by OCLC, must run directly to the modem in the library. Some LECs will run their cable parallel to the in-place cable and terminate it on an extended network interface. The cost of installation and maintenance are included in the LECs regulated charges for the special service circuit. On the other hand, some LECs will accept responsibility for the regulated service beyond the primary network interface (NI) to ensure that a special service circuit performs properly. In such situations they will install a service interface (SI) at the point where the LECs service responsibility ends. The additional cable will either be installed by the LEC on an unregulated basis, or customer-provided cable will be used (i.e., a separation of service responsibility from ownership of the underlying facilities). It is now common practice for LECs to use or even lease wires from customer-owned cables.

Total Service Responsibility

Some information or database service providers (e.g., OCLC) will assume total service responsibility, thus freeing the user under most circumstances from the necessity of having to deal with complex inside-wire issues. Although this inevitably adds an incremental amount to the cost of that service — either directly or indirectly — the economies of scale of such organizations coupled with their experience in dealing with these problems may make the service attractive to the user. In addition, some organizations — particularly colleges and universities — have considerable resident expertise which is available to assist with these decisions.

Potential Health and Liability Problems

Polyvinylchloride (PVC), a plastic insulating material used extensively with telephone wire, may pose serious health and legal liability problems, particularly where PVC-insulated wire has been placed in air-return plenums — ceiling ducts used to circulate air throughout a building. If this wire catches fire, dangerous fumes that can cause lung damage and poisoning can be carried throughout the building.

PVC-insulated telephone wire worth billions of dollars was installed by telephone companies before the danger was recognized about ten years ago. Since PVC-insulated wire is priced at about one-third the cost of flame-resistant wire (e.g., teflon-coated wire), the temptation still exists for users and contractors to continue to install PVC wire. Ownership of, and subsequent liability for, PVC wire installed by telephone companies may have been assumed by users as a result of either recent regulatory actions or the purchase or installation of this wire by the users.

The National Fire Protection Association's (NFPA) National Electrical Code (NEC) banned installation of PVC-insulated wire in air-plenums in 1978. However, the Code is interpreted and enforced differently from state to state and from municipality to municipality. Telephone companies also maintain that a "grandfather clause" protects them from liability for such wire that they may have installed prior to the 1978 ban, but it is not clear whether users who have subsequently assumed ownership are protected by the grandfather clause. A legal spokesman for Illinois Bell Telephone Co., for example, has been quoted as stating, "Wire passed on to users would be a user's responsibility."

The PVC issue has only recently surfaced, and there is continuing controversy with no clear resolution at this time. There remains no doubt that PVC in air plenums is dangerous and potentially fatal. Therefore, the problem should be eliminated, where it exists, as soon as possible, regardless of the legal issues — particularly in public facilities such as libraries. It may also be advantageous for users to take a proactive approach to the PVC problem, planning the systematic removal and replacement of the PVC wire at their convenience, since insurance companies or local inspectors could conceivably mandate immediate removal of the wire in a manner that might prove disruptive to ongoing operations.

It should also be noted that new flame test requirements have recently been developed by the NFPA and Underwriters Laboratories (UL), and incorporated in the NEC. Computer and telephone cable installed after July 1, 1988, must meet the new standards for fire resistance. The new flame-test requirements are some 150 to 200 times more stringent than earlier Appliance Wiring Material, or AWM, requirements. General-purpose cable, connecting computers or telephones between rooms in a building, must meet the new CL2 or CM standards. Riser cable used in vertical shafts must meet CL2R or CMR standards, while Plenum cable used in air ducts must meet CL2P or CMP standards. There is also a restricted use classification (CL2X or CMX) for wire used in short exposed lengths or nonflammable conduit. UL tests cable and lists only cable that meets its standards. Approved cable will bear both the UL logo and the NEC designation.

Summary

The regulatory, judicial, and legislative changes of the last few years have significantly altered the structure of the telecommunications environment, and have led many organizations — particularly library and information related organizations — to the threshold of change. Planning for this change requires a perspective of the changing telecommunications infrastructure, which is discussed in subsequent chapters.

4

"The time has come," the Walrus said, "to talk of many things..."
(Through the Looking Glass) Lewis Carroll [1832–1898]

Telecommunications and Network Technology

This chapter, and the next, provide a broad overview of telecommunications and network-related elements and technologies. Since the objective is to provide a broad technical review, elements most important to general understanding are singled out for discussion at a level consistent with this goal; hence, enabling broader coverage of the field. Some readers will likely find the depth of discussion too superficial, while others may find the breadth of topics covered too narrow. In fact, they will probably both be right; but hopefully many will find the middle ground that the author has endeavored to stake out to be a helpful discussion of a complex and extensive subject.

The use of technical terms and acronyms also presents elements of a dilemma. Clearly, the best approach would be to avoid the slang of the field altogether. This approach would make the material easier to read. Unfortunately, the language of the field is used extensively in many other works. To avoid the language would do a disservice to readers not already familiar with the "words of the trade." Therefore, the author has endeavored to introduce, define, and use many of the terms and acronyms of the field. Although some readers may find this approach annoying, they should recognize the more noble purpose at hand and persevere.

Finally, certain concepts and elements of the technology are fundamentally circular by nature — one can not be appropriately discussed without reference to another. Unfortunately, these can often only be introduced effectively in a serial manner. Although every attempt has been made to avoid this situation, it is not always avoidable; hence, several "forward references" appear in the text. Hopefully, the pieces will all come together in the end.

Network Elements

It is convenient, for purposes of discussion, to categorize the elements of a telecommunications channel into four basic categories:

1. Customer premises equipment (CPE)

2. Access channels

3. Switching equipment and services

4. Long-haul channels

Customer Premises Equipment

Customer premises equipment includes equipment such as private branch exchanges (PBXs), telephone instruments, modems and channel service units (CSUs), data terminal equipment, facsimile terminals, automatic call directors (ACDs), network-attached alarm and surveillance equipment, answering machines, etc., all located on the subscriber's premises. CSUs are the digital-service equivalent of analog modems. ACDs are devices, such as those often used by reservation services, that automatically answer incoming calls and route them to the next available of several attendants. This equipment is often collectively called simply terminal equipment, since it is the equipment upon which the communications channel terminates.

Access Channels

Access channels, which are used to connect the local subscribers' equipment to the long-distance network, include primarily:

1. Switched access channels (i.e., local-loop facilities)

2. Special access channels used with private lines, WATS lines, etc., that do not use the local telephone company's switching equipment

3. Subscriber acquired and/or provided facilities (e.g., bypass facilities)

Access channels are sometimes also called first mile/last mile facilities.

Switching Equipment and Services

Switching equipment and services include the equipment within the public network necessary to route, measure, account for, and otherwise handle local and long-distance calls, including services such as Centrex (discussed elsewhere in this book) provided by the local exchange carrier (LEC). Private voice and/or data networks may also employ switching equipment. Private voice-network switching equipment typically consist of two or more PBXs interconnected using private-line or bypass facilities. Private data networks usually consists of similarly interconnected data-switching equipment, such as computers or packet-switching nodes.

In larger networks, so-called tandem switches may also be found. A tandem switch usually denotes switching between backbone trunks, as compared with the switching functions necessary to connect access lines to the long-distance trunks. A typical tandem network configuration might be several remote PBXs interconnected, respectively, via private trunks to the nearest signal transfer point (STP) on the private tandem network. The trunks would then be appropriately switched over the tandem network to the similarly connected destination PBX. Data switches can similarly utilize a tandem network, and it is not unusual to find both voice and data switches passing traffic simultaneously over such high-capacity tandem backbone networks.

Switching elements can generally be categorized into three types: circuit switching, message switching, and packet switching. A circuit-switching device establishes a dedicated connection between two user elements on a network (e.g., between two telephone instruments). A message switch does not require a direct and immediate connection between such elements. Messages are queued for the various recipients and delivered at some future time. Examples of message switching might be Telex, electronic mail, or voice-mail messaging. This can enable more efficient use of transmission facilities, and allows communications between elements which may not be simultaneously present on the network. The important distinction between a message switch and a circuit switch is that information passes nearly instantaneously between originating and terminating elements using a circuit switch, while significant delays may result from message switching. For this reason, real-time, online interactive communications usually favor the use of circuit over message switching.

Packet switching has many of the advantages of both circuit and message switching. Packet-switching systems break incoming messages into small "packets" — usually no more than 128 characters — and more-or-less immediately deliver the partial messages to another switch where the message is reassembled and delivered to the intended receiving station. A typical packet-switching network can deliver a packet of information in a fraction of a second and, therefore, can accommodate a large number of real-time users on a shared basis, each with relatively low data throughput requirements. This allows the network to achieve a high level of utilization of the transmission facilities. Packets may be relayed between several nodes on a network before reaching their final destination. Most often, the actual path the various packets follow through the packet network is identical for each packet, however, it is possible to allow each packet to flow on a separate and often dynamically determined path. This can enhance both the security of messages as well as the efficiency of network facilities used. Unfortunately, it can also substantially increase overhead in the network processors, and complicate recovery from failures.

Long-Haul Facilities

Long-haul facilities consist of those facilities that provide transmission of information between local access and transport areas (LATAs). These may be either public network facilities, provided by one of the several public interexchange carriers (IXCs) such as AT&T, MCI, or US Sprint, or possibly private facilities, such as private fiber-optic or microwave-radio circuits. Satellite space segment — the satellite link between earthstations — is also considered a long-haul facility.

Analog and Digital Signals

Telecommunications involves the transmission of information that can be transmitted in either analog or digital form. Analog signals vary continuously while digital signals consist of a series of discrete elements that take on one, and only one value at a time. Although voice is usually thought of as being transmitted as an analog signal, as compared with computer data, that is usually thought of as a digital signal; both voice and data are forms of information that can be transmitted either as digital or analog signals. It is possible to convert between signal forms, and typically the nature of transmission on any segment of a network is determined by physical limitations or the cost of the transmission system.

Historically, most transmission systems have been analog; however, many modern transmission and switching systems are digital in nature. A key advantage of digital transmission systems over analog systems is that digital signals are simpler and less costly to regenerate over long distances, whereas the repeated amplification of analog signals amplifies any extraneous noise along with the original signal — something digital regeneration does not do.

Bandwidth

The range of frequencies a telecommunications channel can transmit is called its bandwidth. Mathematically, it is the difference of the highest and the lowest frequency (i.e., the lower frequency subtracted from the higher frequency), and is usually quoted in Hertz (Hz), which is numerically the same as cycles per second. The capacity of a channel to carry information is directly related to its bandwidth. Since a channel can only carry, or pass, signals within its bandwidth, this is often described as the bandpass of the channel.

Voice/Data Systems

As the cost and size of digital technology have decreased significantly, it has become more attractive to digitize data, voice, and even video, at the source. These can then be transmitted as bit streams and reconstructed at the receiving end with significant improvement in quality of the transmission. End-to-end digital transmission has led to the emergence of integrated communications systems to support integrated voice/data processing.

Pulse Code Modulation

The most common form of speech digitization is associated with pulse code modulation (PCM). Using PCM, the voice signal is sampled (i.e., measured) 8,000 times each second, with each sample being encoded into 8 bits of digital information. This yields a 64 Kbps, or thousand bits per second (i.e., $8,000 \times 8 = 64,000$) bit stream. Algorithms have been developed that allow voice to be transmitted at lower data rates. Adaptive differential pulse code modulation (ADPCM), which transmits at an effective 32 Kbps, transmits the changes between successive samples, rather than the sample value itself, resulting in about half as much data. Since the human ear perceives volume differences differently at different volume levels (i.e., non-linearly), several algorithms are also employed to take advantage of this fact in the digitization process.

Packet-Voice Techniques

Only about 22% of a voice signal consists of essential speech components. The remainder is mostly silent periods or pauses, background noise, and redundant repetitive pitch patterns. The potential exists for significant improvements in transmission efficiency by packetizing the digital voice elements and transmitting only these useful data elements over the channel; thus enabling productive use of the channel to carry additional traffic during the time periods it otherwise would not be carrying productive traffic. Unlike more conventional techniques, packet-voice techniques do not establish dedicated bandwidth circuits for a given call, but rather share the available bandwidth.

Integration and Consolidation

Integration of communication facilities has other advantages as well. The potential for improvements in both economies of scale and efficiency of utilization of integrated facilities can be a major consideration. Overhead for support and maintenance of several different networks can be reduced through consolidation. On the other hand, voice and data can have very different requirements — differences, such as those discussed later in this book, that may not be effectively accommodated, either technically or economically, using currently available technology. Advances in modern technology are, however, reducing or eliminating these potential constraints in many instances.

Fortunately, it is possible to bring about integration and consolidation of voice and data traffic at different levels within a network hierarchy. This might be accomplished at the lowest level using an integrated (i.e., voice/data) digital PBX connected to digital transmission facilities. It can also be accomplished by bringing together separate local voice and data networks (e.g., a PBX with the capability to accommodate digital trunks and a local area data network) to consolidate transmission on a single digital long-distance network; thus taking advantage of consolidation on the long-distance facilities.

At a still higher level, several digital transmission channels can be brought together and consolidated at an intermediate location, carried from that location on high-capacity digital trunks, and shed again as separate digital channels at distant locations. This can be an effective way for several different organizations or institutions to consolidate traffic and take advantage of the resulting economies of scale — particularly where there exists a significant volume of traffic between two or more of the various institutions. This is often called tandem networking, since it takes advantage of two or more digital switching devices interconnected to backbone circuits in tandem (i.e., in such a way as to provide switching functions between backbone trunks).

It is important to note that the various channels may be truly integrated, where traffic originating on one logical network or channel might terminate on another, or simply consolidated, where a logical channel appears to be distinct and separate, even though it may have traveled as part of a larger digital transmission channel at some point in the network. An analogy might be a bridge over a river that carries traffic from two separate highways. Traffic from both roads may be merged onto a single roadway over the bridge (i.e., integration) or two separate roadways might be maintained using the same support structure (i.e., consolidation). This can be a subtle distinction, but is important since true integration typically provides the opportunity for more efficient utilization of the respective long-haul facility, as well as facilitates interconnectivity of user stations. Therefore, whether through consolidation or integration, it can be advantageous to build networks of networks in this manner. The evolving National Science Foundation network (NSFNET) is an important example of such a network concept.

Serial and Parallel Transmission

Most computers and other computer-based equipment handle digital data internally in groups of bits (e.g., often 8 bits, or a byte at a time, or in multiples of 8-bit bytes). It is convenient for these devices to present internal data to the external environment a byte at a time. This is typically the way data are communicated, for example, between a computer and a high-speed printer. The various bits of the byte travel along parallel circuits, and are said to be transmitted in parallel. Interfaces that accommodate this mechanism are said to be parallel interfaces. Often external devices (e.g., modems) can only accommodate data a single bit at a time. When this is the case, it is necessary to transmit the various bits that comprise the byte in a serial fashion, one after the other over a single channel. This gives rise to the term serial transmission, and such an interface is called a serial interface. There are many commercially available devices that perform the conversion between serial and parallel modes of transmission; these are called parallel to serial converters. In the personal computer environment, these are often called communications boards, or COM ports. Although seldom thought of in these terms, parallel to serial conversion is actually an application of time-division multiplexing discussed later in this chapter.

Synchronous and Asynchronous Transmission

It is necessary that the transmitting and receiving devices on a telecommunications channel be synchronized in time if they are to pass data successfully. There are two methods of accomplishing this in common practice; namely, synchronous mode and asynchronous mode. In synchronous mode, the transmitting device sends special characters (called "synch" characters) at the beginning of a message, and then sends the entire message in a continuous sequence — much like soldiers marching in single file. This obviously requires a reasonably sophisticated device at both the sending and receiving end. By contrast, asynchronous mode frames each character with a special "start bit" and one or more special "stop bits," which are recognized by both the sending and receiving devices. Since the characters can be sent one at a time when the device is ready to send them, far less sophistication is required of the device. Also, in synchronous mode only two synch characters need to be added to the entire message — although three or four are commonly sent for redundancy; while in asynchronous mode, two or three bits are added to each character. Therefore, it is more efficient to transmit in synchronous mode, with the exception of very short (e.g., about eight characters or fewer) messages. Typically some sort of transmission error detection information is also appended to the synchronous data block (i.e., message).

Data Service Units/Channel Service Units

As noted earlier, transmission of information can take two forms, analog or digital. It is, however, possible to convert from one form to the other. If a digital transmission mechanism (e.g., AT&T Dataphone Digital Service, or DDS) is used, then devices generating digital data (e.g., data terminals or computers) typically connect to the digital network using a data service unit/channel service unit (DSU/CSU) arrangement. The DSU is essentially a short-distance, synchronous data line driver, and a CSU is an access arrangement that provides local-loop equalization (discussed later in this chapter), protection from electrical transients (e.g., dangerous voltage spikes, etc.), circuit isolation and testing capabilities. In most jurisdictions, a customer can furnish both the DSU and the CSU, making a combined unit most economically attractive. Separate DSUs and CSUs are available where the local telephone company insists on supplying the CSU. Unlike the analog case, the data clock, which is the timing mechanism by which the value of the data elements are determined upon receipt, is supplied by the digital transmission system — not the customer device. This can give rise to timing incompatibilities when data is passed from one digital transmission system to another. These problems, which frequently arise when users attempt to interconnect different digital networks, can usually be overcome by using a data buffering device to temporarily hold the incoming data bits until the outgoing device can transmit them. The important point is that the user be aware of this potential timing problem.

Modems

When the transmission channel is analog in nature (e.g., local switched telephone network or analog private leased lines), some device is required to translate between the digital data produced by digital devices and the analog transmission system. Since the transmission channel has a bandwidth determined by the channel itself, the typical translation device produces one (or more) analog signals, well within the limits of the bandwidth, called carrier signals. The frequencies of these carrier signals are, as might be expected, called the carrier frequencies. The digital data is then appropriately encoded and imposed on the carrier. This process is called modulation of the carrier signal. The reverse process is accomplished at the receiver end, where the carrier signal is demodulated and the data decoded and presented to the digital equipment in digital form. The process of *mod*ulation/*dem*odulation gives rise to the name "modem" for these devices. Unlike the digital case, the signal timing element is generated by the modem, although in some special circumstances it is provided to the modem by an external source (e.g., a DSU/CSU when the analog channel is used as an extension of a digital circuit). It should be noted that the modem-to-modem connection is inherently asymmetric, since the carrier frequency used to transmit from one end must be the same frequency used to receive at the other. A different frequency is used for the return path. For this reason it is necessary for the modem device to know whether it is an originating device or an answering device — the two names typically used to distinguish between the two ends. On private networks, these are often called "master" and "slave" modems.

Modulation Techniques

A variety of mechanisms are employed to modulate the analog carrier — too many and too complex to describe and discuss within the limits of this chapter. In general, either the amplitude of the carrier is modulated (i.e., amplitude modulation, or AM), the frequency of the carrier is modulated (i.e., frequency modulation, or FM), or the phase of the carrier signal is modulated (i.e., phase modulation, or PM). Often the frequency or the phase is abruptly shifted, giving rise to so-called frequency-shift keying (FSK) or phase-shift keying (PSK). Sometimes more than one of the carrier's parameters are simultaneously varied.

Baud, Bits per Second, and Symbols

A source of confusion, even among some telecommunications professionals, concerns "baud" rates and "bit" rates. A baud is one signal element per second, often referred to as a line transition. One bit per second (bps) refers to the transmission of one bit of binary data in one second. It should be noted that a baud and a bps are not necessarily numerically the same, although they may be the same. Using modern modulation techniques, it is possible — and in fact common — to encode more than one bit of data into a single signal element, called a symbol. It is not unusual for modern sophisticated equipment to encode five or more bits of information in a single signal element. Although discussion of the detailed theory and engineering associated with these techniques is not appropriate for a general overview treatises, Table 1 lists several of these commonly used analog modulation techniques, their corresponding logical levels, and the number of bits encoded in each symbol (or element referenced by a baud).

Table 1
Modulation Techniques, Levels, and Bits per Symbol

Type of Modulation	Logical Levels	Bits per Symbol
Amplitude Modulation (AM)	2	1
Frequency-Shift Keying (FSK)	2	1
Phase-Shift Keying (PSK)		
— 2 phase	2	1
Phase-Shift Keying (PSK)		
— 4 phase	4	2
Phase-Shift Keying (PSK)		
— 8 phase	8	3
Phase-Shift Keying (PSK)		
— 16 phase	16	4
Quadrature Partial Response		
Signaling AM (16-point)	16	4
Quadrature Partial Response		
Signaling AM (32-point)	32	5

Therefore, baud is a measure of the rate at which signal elements are flowing, while bps is a measure of the rate at which bits of data are flowing; these are often not the same. Unless there is an engineering purpose related to the use of the term baud, it is recommended that the term bps be habitually used to indicate digital data rate.

Channel Capacity

A leased or switched communication circuit represents a financial investment, therefore it is only natural to ask how much information can be transmitted over a specified circuit. Answering this question is not simple, and a rigorous treatment involves complex mathematics; however, the basic concepts and results are not difficult to comprehend on an intuitive level.

The amount of data that can be transmitted is directly related to the bandwidth available to be used. It is not surprising that the maximum bps is also related to the power of the transmitter as compared with the noise signals which inevitably occur on the circuit. It is also not surprising that the result of attempting to push too much data through a circuit is that errors occur. Since the symbols can interfere with one another, it is advantageous to encode multiple bits in each symbol. Using reasonable assumptions about the parameters of a typical long-distance telephone line (i.e., voice frequency analog channel, or 3002 VFC — the type used by OCLC on its dedicated network), Table 2 relates the theoretical maximum channel capacity in bps for several values of bits per symbol.

Table 2
Bits per Symbol, Levels, and Channel Capacity

Bits per Symbol	Logical Levels	Channel Capacity
1	2	6,300 bps
2	4	12,600 bps
3	8	18,900 bps
4	16	25,200 bps
5	32	31,500 bps

Although the data rates listed above are theoretically possible, in practice modern technology has not progressed to allow dependable transmission at these rates; however, commercial products are readily available that permit transmission at rates of 19.2 Kbps over a similar channel. These rates are expected to increase with the implementation of increasingly more powerful computer-based circuitry in modem equipment. The typical trade-off criteria involves the point at which it becomes less expensive to lease another channel, as compared with investment in more expensive modem equipment. The OCLC dedicated network encodes two bits, called a dibit, in each symbol and transmits at a rate of 2.4 Kbps (i.e., 1,200 baud).

Data and Clock Recovery

If incoming data streams are to be detected and decoded, it is necessary that the receiver posses accurate and specific timing information. This is because data is transmitted by establishing a correlation between the specific state of the channel and a specific time reference. Therefore, the data can be detected and decoded from the channel only if this time reference is known to the receiver. This signal timing element, called the data clock, is most often extracted from the transmitted signal itself. The engineering techniques by which this is accomplished are complex, and are discussed elsewhere. Of interest here is the fact that the clock signal is necessary to the detection and decoding of the received signal, and that this clock can be effectively derived from the incoming signals themselves.

Short-Haul Transmission Devices

Short-haul transmission devices are generally used with inexpensive 2- and 4-wire twisted-pair wire (i.e., ordinary telephone wiring). They are often used within a building or local complex. Depending on the type of wire used, ranges of from a few thousand feet to several miles are possible. Range usually depends on the data rate, transmission mode, and the phone line, as well as the transmitting and receiving devices. In general, lines obtained from the phone company are not suitable for short-haul devices (e.g., they frequently use devices designed to facilitate voice transmission, such as so-called loading coils). In some cases, it is possible to special order phone company lines that have no filters or transformers, permitting the wider bandwidth necessary to support the typically wider frequency spectrum that short-haul devices require — particularly at 9.6 Kbps and higher. The phone company may also place limits on the power levels and frequency ranges carried by these lines, to prevent interference with other subscribers. This can lower both the distance and speed of data transmissions.

Short-haul products come in a variety of types. These range from basic line drivers (e.g., cable extenders) which are essentially interface converters that change the interface signals to a low voltage, low impedance format more suited to the line characteristics discussed elsewhere in this chapter. Typically the binary nature of the data is not altered, so line drivers are not data code or protocol sensitive.

Transmission Media

The various transmission media typically found in telecommunications systems present different characteristics and capacities, and include:

- Twisted-pair cable

- Coaxial cable

- Radio waves

- Microwave radio and infrared light

- Satellites

- Waveguides

- Optical fibers

Twisted-Pair Cable

Relatively low in cost, twisted-pair cables support a limited bandwidth. Twisted-pair wire is typically used to carry a single voice or data circuit up to a practical maximum of about 14,400 bps over distances of up to a few miles. It is also used to carry up to 24 (i.e., PCM), and sometimes up to 44 (i.e., ADPCM) digital voice channels between telephone company, or equivalent equipment (i.e., T-1 facilities, discussed elsewhere in this chapter).

Coaxial Cable

Coaxial cable, probably most familiar from cable-television distribution systems, has the capacity to support the equivalent of up to 13,200 voice channels in the telephone network, with repeating amplifiers typically required about every mile. The medium is often used in local area networks (LANs) that typically carry up to 10 million bps (Mbps), with some systems operating at 80 Mbps or more.

Radio Waves

Radio waves have been used as a medium for communication since shortly after they were discovered by Heinrich Hertz in 1889. Guglielmo Marconi demonstrated the first mobile radio in 1898. Today, the term radio wave is generally used for that part of the electromagnetic spectrum with frequencies of less than about a

GHz (i.e., billion Hertz); emanations that do not exhibit the propagation character-istics of light waves to any considerable extent. Above these frequencies lie the microwave, millimeter, and infrared light portions of the electromagnetic spectrum that are also of importance to telecommunications.

Radio waves are commonly used for applications ranging from cordless telephones, to mobile and marine telephones, paging systems, train– and air-to-ground communications, and packet-radio networks. There is also an evolving application of radio to provide basic telephone service in rural areas (e.g., basic exchange telephone radio, or BETR).

Microwave Radio and Infrared Light

Most commonly used for long-distance circuits in the telephone system, microwave radio is also used for local television links and private telecommunica-tions systems. Like coaxial cable, microwave links can carry a large number of telephone circuits with 6,000 per channel not uncommon. Unlike coaxial cable however, microwave must have a direct line-of-sight between towers which must be located every 25–30 miles or so (due primarily to the curvature of the earth). Microwave links are subject to interference from such things as snow and rain, although accommodation of these elements is usually made as a part of the design of the systems. While existing interexchange carrier microwave systems are ex-pected to be upgraded and enhanced where needed, construction of new systems will gradually decrease over the next five years due to competition from fiber-optic systems. US Sprint recently announced its intent to sell its microwave and satellite network with the completion of its fiber-optic network. Infrared light (IR), similar to microwaves, is often used to transmit signals over short distances, but is much more sensitive to the effects of fog, rain and snow.

Satellites

Satellites can be thought of as microwave repeaters usually located in appar-ently stationary orbit (i.e., geostationary orbit; having an orbital period of 24 hours about the equator) about 22,300 miles above the surface of the earth, and commonly carry up to 21,600 or more voice-circuit equivalents. Since the time for a signal traveling to and from a satellite at the speed of light is about a quarter-second (i.e., about one-eighth of a second to or from the satellite; a half-second circuit-round-trip, end-to-end), use of satellite links for voice conversations can be annoying, and the delay can be intolerable for certain types of computer communications. In addition, satellites may also be bothered by interference caused by solar radiation during certain periods of the year as they cross the disk of the sun as viewed from earth. Using microwave technology, they are also subject to the same interference effects.

Waveguides

Waveguides are nothing more than "microwave pipes" used to transmit micro-wave signals, and commonly support up to 230,000 voice circuit equivalents. They are typically not used in private systems, and have been all but supplanted by modern fiber-optic technology. Waveguides are often used to transmit microwave signals up and down microwave antenna towers.

Optical Fibers

Optical fibers, one of the newest transmission media, are hair-thin glass (or other optically conducting) filaments with the capacity to transmit extremely large quantities of information. More than 6.8 million miles of optical fiber have been installed worldwide, and the annual rate of installation growth is over 80%. Limitations on fiber-optic systems are currently imposed by the transmitting and receiving systems, and not the media itself. This is typically a result of the necessity to convert between electronic and light signals; however much effort is currently being expended to produce practical photonic circuitry that would deal directly with the optical signals. In fact, AT&T Bell Laboratories recently built an $85-million, 450,000-square-foot facility in Breigingsville, Pennsylvania, that will employ 800 scientists, engineers and staff, for the specific purpose of conducting fundamental and applied research on photonics, the technology of using light to carry information. Current commercial systems typically operate at up to 565 Mbps, but an experimental system has been demonstrated to operate at 20 billion bps, or Gbps (i.e., more than a 35-fold increase) over a distance of more than 40 miles. Nominal operating capacity of commercial systems is expected to increase from the current typical 565 Mbps to 1.2 to 1.7 Gbps by 1989, and increase further to around 6 Gbps by 1995. The cost of optical fiber has decreased by nearly tenfold since 1980.

Transmission Characteristics

Telecommunications involves the transmission of signals from one point to another. Inherent in this process are extraneous noise signals and other phenomenon that must be overcome if the information contained in the transmitted signals is to be correctly interpreted at the destination point. Noise, in its broadest sense, consists of any undesirable signal in a communications circuit, and it is noise that is the major limiting factor in telecommunication system performance. Noise can arise both external and internal to the transmission medium itself, and as a consequence of the transmission of the signals themselves. It can be generally divided into four categories:

1.   Thermal noise

2.   Intermodulation noise

3.   Crosstalk

4.   Impulse noise

Thermal Noise

Thermal noise is a general expression for noise signals which arise from the thermal agitation (i.e., the movement of electrons due to thermal causes) of the media, and is present in all transmission channels. Intermodulation and crosstalk result from undesirable interactions of transmitted signals, either between signal elements on a given channel or between signal elements on adjacent channels. Impulse noise arises from sources external to the channel.

Signal-to-Noise Ratio

The most common transmission criteria with which the telecommunications engineer must deal is the signal-to-noise ratio. For this reason, this term is frequently encountered by users in specifications for transmission and related equipment. This ratio expresses the amount by which a signal level exceeds its underlying noise. In other words, the signal-to-noise ratio can be thought of as an indication of how easily the transmitted information can be distinguished from the accompanying noise — the understandability of the received signals.

Attenuation

Electrical signals become weaker, or are attenuated, as they move through a cable. Since radio, microwave, infrared and light waves are all forms of electromagnetic radiation, they are also subject to attenuation. In a cable, the rate of attenuation is a function of both physical characteristics (e.g., cable size, geometry, material type, etc.) and of the frequency of the signal. In general for electrical signals, attenuation increases in proportion to the length of the cable and decreases in proportion to an increase in the cross-sectional area of the conducting medium. It also increases with increasing frequency of the signal. Therefore, the longer the cable, the smaller the conductor, and the higher the signal frequency, the weaker will be the received signal. As the received signal becomes weaker in relation to the inherent noise, the smaller will be the signal-to-noise ratio, and the more difficult it becomes to accurately determine the information content of the received signals.

Attenuation Distortion

Since digital telecommunications signals often take the form of "square waves," so called since a graph of the signal amplitude over time assumes the shape of a square, and since these waves are actually composed of electrical signals (i.e., sine waves) of many frequencies, the selective attenuation of higher frequency components of the square wave distorts the shape of the wave as it traverses the length of the cable. The result is that the sharp corners of the square waves become rounded and the form of the square becomes elongated, making it more difficult to determine where one pulse ends and the next pulse begins (Figure 1). This puts a limit on how close together the original pulses can occur on the given cable. Obviously, this limits how much data can be transmitted in a given unit of time. It should also be noted that the same phenomenon occurs with analog signal forms, but the consequences are not as easily visualized — although the end result is the same. In both cases, the level of distinguishable signal in relation to the underlying noise is decreased — i.e., the signal-to-noise ratio is decreased.

Dispersion

The velocity of propagation of electrical signals in conducting media also varies with the frequency of the signal. This is equally true in optical conductors as in electrical conductors. Just as attenuation at different rates for different component frequencies of a transmitted signal can result in distortion of that signal, the fact that different frequency components travel at different velocities in a cable, a phenomenon called dispersion, likewise results in distortion of the signal, and places a limit on the data capacity of the cable. Again, the signal-to-noise ratio is decreased.

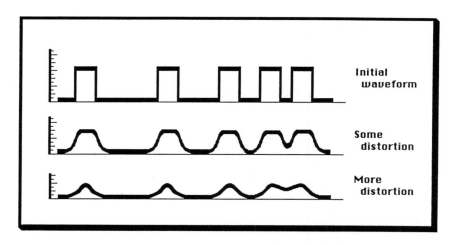

Figure 1 Distortion "Smears" Waveform and Limits Channel Speed

Multipath Distortion

It is often possible for a transmitted signal to take different physical paths between the transmitter and the receiver, a phenomenon called multipath distortion. Examples might include radio transmissions that may follow both a direct path and a path that might involve being reflected from a tall building, etc., or a light pulse in certain optical fibers (e.g., so-called multimode fibers) that may follow both a direct path down the center of the cable, and be bounced back and forth experiencing many reflections from the wall of the fiber on its journey through the fiber. This can result in paths of different lengths through the channel, and hence the signal arriving at slightly different times at the receiver. The result is that the received signal pulse can become distorted, with the signal element boundaries being spread out in time; the signal elements become less distinguishable, the data capacity is restricted, and the signal-to-noise ratio decreased.

Intersymbol Interference

The phenomenon of one signal pulse interfering with another is called inter-symbol interference, or intermodulation noise. Although the end result of anomalous attenuation (i.e., attenuation as a function of frequency), anomalous dispersion (i.e., changes in signal velocity as a function of frequency) and multipath distortion is the same, namely distortion of the transmitted signal and a limit on the transmission capacity of the cable, the phenomena are physically very different. Of importance is the fact that the transmitted signal will change in both strength and form as it traverses the length of a cable. In practical applications, a certain degree of compensation can be made for these effects, hence improving the characteristics of the related transmission facility.

Crosstalk

Frequently a transmission cable contains more than one signal path. If the cable is not properly designed and constructed, or if the strength of the transmitted signal carried by one or more of the paths is excessive, it is possible for the signal in one path to "escape" onto another transmission path. This is called crosstalk. In order to minimize this effect, each wire pair in a properly designed and constructed twisted-pair cable will have a different twist rate (i.e., number of twists per inch). Shielding the cable (i.e., surrounding it with a protective conductor, often consisting of metallic foil) will also reduce the incidence of crosstalk, as well as noise from other external sources.

External Noise

It is also possible for externally originating electrical interference, or impulse noise, to find its way onto a transmission cable. This is often caused by the presence of proximate building electrical wiring, or other electrical equipment (e.g., large elevator motors, fluorescent lights, etc.). This interference can be minimized by avoiding running transmission cables near such potential sources of interference, or by shielding the cable as previously discussed. Compensation can also sometimes be made for persistent interference of this kind by the use of electrical filtering, which is discussed later in this chapter.

Ground Loops

An often particularly troublesome and misunderstood source of external noise is caused by so-called ground loops. The electric power distribution system often uses the earth itself as a return path to the generator source for electric power circuits. If an electrically conducting telecommunications cable is connected to an electrical ground at both ends (i.e., potentially different grounds), these utility power return currents often find the telecommunications cable a convenient path to follow for a part of their return journey, and sizable unwanted electrical currents can result. This phenomenon, which often results when shielding conductors are connected to grounds at both ends of the cable, can be easily avoided by simply assuring that telecommunications cables are not connected to multiple grounds. Such ground loops can also be eliminated by the use of isolation circuitry.

Characteristic Impedance

The characteristic impedance of a transmission facility, although sometimes complex to calculate in practice, is not conceptually difficult to understand. Most are familiar with the concept of electrical resistance; the property of electrical conductors to oppose the flow of electric currents. For steady-state (i.e., direct current) electrical currents, impedance and resistance are equivalent. However, as the frequency of an electrical signal increases, the opposition to flow of electrical currents, called impedance, can change. The characteristic impedance of a properly designed transmission cable is independent of cable length. The key issue with characteristic impedance is to have uniform impedance in any given cable. Improperly matched impedances, resulting from connections to the cable or the splicing together of dissimilar cables, results in electrical reflections in the cable that can seriously affect transmission performance. That is, such points of abrupt change in characteristic impedance can act in a manner similar to a mirror that reflects light.

Amplification and Regeneration

As previously discussed, distortion of transmitted signals can occur as they propagate through various transmission facilities. Several techniques are employed to compensate for these detrimental effects. Simple attenuation (i.e., the decrease in signal strength) can be partially overcome through the use of signal amplifiers. Unfortunately, analog amplifiers not only amplify the transmitted signal, but also any extraneous noise or signal distortion that might have occurred as well. Digital signal amplification, called signal regeneration, does not suffer this problem so long as the incoming signal is sufficiently clear as to be unambiguously regenerated and retransmitted.

Filtering and Equalization

Since distortion is more or less constant and characteristic of the specific transmission facility, its effects are often predictable, and compensation can be made to reduce these effects. The presence of a systematic noise signal (e.g., a 60 Hz signal from an unavoidable proximate power distribution cable or motor) can be removed, or at least greatly reduced, by selective electrical filtering. The effects of other forms of distortion can also be greatly reduced. The idea is to purposely distort the signal in such a way as to exactly offset, or counteract, the characteristic distortion of the signal that occurs on the transmission channel. This can take place at the transmitting source, the receiving (or intermediate amplification) point, or both. When this is accomplished at the transmitting end of a cable section, it is called pulse shaping, and when it is accomplished at the receiving end, it is called equalization.

In the past, filtering, pulse shaping, and equalization have been necessarily carried out with simple passive circuits, or at most, relatively simple electronic circuitry, because of cost and size limitations. For these reasons, seldom has any attempt been made to change the compensation characteristics based upon the dynamic characteristics of the signals and cable (e.g., different channels, or changes in a channel over time). Compensation on a given channel was static once the design point had been determined and the appropriate compensator installed and tuned. With the advent of modern, very powerful, very small, and relatively cheap computer technology, these limitations no longer apply. It is now possible to construct very powerful, small and cheap devices that have the capability to dynamically structure the appropriate compensation depending upon the specific characteristics of the channel. Thus, dynamic line equalization and dynamic line filtering devices are available, based on very large scale integrated (VLSI) circuits, that are small, effective, and relatively cheap.

Echo Cancellation

When a communications channel is used to carry information in both directions (e.g., a long-distance telephone call), it is possible for some of the transmitted signal to be reflected back to the originating end, either from the far receiving end, or from some intermediary amplifier or connection point. This can be annoying for human conversations, and potentially devastating for data traffic. Many modern modems posses the capability to detect and cancel these echoes. This technique is called "echo cancellation," or "dynamic echo cancellation" when this is done dynamically. If echo cancellation is present external to the modem device (e.g., using a long-distance dial-access connection), the network-resident echo cancellation can sometimes interfere with the transmission of data. It is sometimes possible for transmitting devices to generate control signals that instruct the network equipment to turn off network-resident echo cancellation processes.

Multiplexing

Typically, telecommunications channels are valuable and limited resources. For this reason, a primary objective of telecommunications management is to make optimum use of the existing capacity while maintaining acceptable levels of performance. There are also significant economies of scale involved with telecommunications channels. Larger capacity facilities generally present significant per-unit-capacity cost advantages (i.e., are usually priced cheaper than smaller channels on a unit-capacity basis). Various multiplexing techniques are commonly employed to bring different traffic together to both develop economies of scale and enable optimum utilization of the available channel.

Multiplexing is, therefore, a method of transmitting two or more separate channels on a single transmission facility. There are several different techniques commonly used to accomplish this end:

1. Frequency-division multiplexing (FDM)

2. Time-division multiplexing (TDM)

3. Statistical multiplexing

Frequency-division Multiplexing

Frequency-division multiplexing divides the bandwidth of the channel into two or more subchannels. A common example of a FDM facility is the AM radio band in any major city, the capacity of which is divided into many separate channels that are simultaneously used by the various AM radio stations.

Time-division Multiplexing

Time-division multiplexing divides the channel by time, rather than bandwidth, giving each subchannel use of the respective facility on a one-by-one basis. Both FDM and TDM techniques, in and of themselves, simply enable combination and subsequent separation of the various subchannels, but make no attempt to further optimize channel utilization.

Statistical Multiplexing

Frequently, the nature of communications produce traffic patterns that are "bursty" or intermittent in nature, hence much of the multiplexed channel capacity remains underutilized. Statistical multiplexing techniques attempt to allocate channel capacity on the basis of transmission of productive traffic. In addition, some systems attempt to remove or reduce redundant information. These so-called compression techniques may achieve an apparent improvement in information throughput on a communications channel by processing the information in this manner prior to transmission and subsequently reconstructing the original information pattern at the receiving end.

T-Carrier and DS1 Multiplexing

A commonly used format for high-speed data transmission is the Bell DS1 standard transmitted over T-1 facilities. T-1 facilities have attained a particularly prominent role in modern networking. Private-line services presently account for more than $7 billion in revenue nationwide. The demand for private T-1 lines currently represents approximately 10% of this market. Although originally designed to handle digitized voice at a composite rate of 1.544 Mbps, T-1 also transmits multiplexed data.

The DS1 standard not only specifies a transmission rate, but also a specific multiplexing format. The North American (AT&T) D1D DS1 PCM format calls for a frame of 24 eight-bit bytes (i.e., one byte per frame for each of the 24 multiplexed voice circuits), plus a variable framing bit (i.e., "S" bit) making a total of 193 bits per frame. 8,000 frames are transmitted each second, which results in a convenient sampling rate for digitizing voice channels. Hence, 193 bits transmitted 8,000 times per second yields the 1.544 Mbps rate. A superframe consists of 12 frames, and the S bit in each frame is set to identify the superframe through the unique framing pattern "000110111001" (Figure 2). Although it is commonly stated that each digital voice channel has 64 Kbps of channel capacity (i.e., 8 bits transmitted 8,000 times per second, or 64,000 bps), this is not strictly the case. In the D1D format, bit 8 of each byte of the 6th and 12th frame is "robbed" by the network to transmit signaling information (i.e., in-band signaling, which is discussed later).

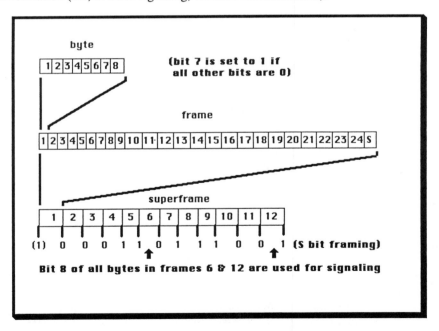

Figure 2 North American (AT&T) D1D DS1 **PCM** Frame Structure

Since a 0 bit results in no pulse being transmitted, while a 1 bit results in alternately positive and negative pulses (i.e., negative if the last pulse was positive, and visa versa), a string of 0s results in no pulses being available to the receiver to maintain the integrity of the receive signal element (i.e., receive clock, discussed elsewhere in this chapter). This is avoided by substituting a 1 bit in bit-position 7 of all digital voice data bytes that would otherwise have all bits equal to 0 (i.e., the channel bank equipment actually changes the data).

When T-1 is used for data (i.e., AT&T Dataphone Digital Service, or DDS), only 56 Kbps of the 64 Kbps multiplexed channel are available to the user. The 1.544 Mbps line speed, as applied to DDS service, has the same frame and superframe structure as discussed above. The DDS format, however, calls for one bit of each 8-bit byte (i.e., "C" bit) to be reserved for network use; hence, 7 user bits times 8,000 frames per second yields a basic DDS channel speed of 56 Kbps. The encoding of the C bit in the data application is structured to avoid long strings of "0" bits, which are common in data applications. It should also be noted that this eliminates the possibility of an all 0 byte, and hence the situation of 1-bit insertion never becomes a problem. Unfortunately, this is accomplished at the expense of user bandpass.

It should be noted that the Bell DS1 standard is not a universally accepted international standard, and elsewhere around the world the comparable facilities transmit at an aggregate rate of 2.048 Mbps (i.e., Conference Europenne des Postes et Telecommunications, or CEPT 30 + 2 system). In this format, 30 of the 32 frames are dedicated to the user, while the remaining two are reserved for signaling (i.e., out-of-band signaling), which accommodates 30 truly 64 Kbps user channels. This can give rise to compatibility problems with DS1/T-1 for international communications. AT&T is, however, currently considering several comparable new service offerings that would be compatible with the European standards. In addition to T-1, there exists a hierarchy of North American T-carrier facilities. These include T-1, T-1C, T-2, T-3, and T-4, and range in capacity from 1.544 Mbps to 274.176 Mbps as illustrated in Table 3.

Table 3
U.S. T-Carrier Digital Transmission Hierarchy

T-Carrier Level	Data Rate (Mbps)	Number of Phone Lines Multiplexed
T-1 (DS1)	1.544	24
T-1C (DS1C)	3.152	48
T-2 (DS2)	6.312	96
T-3 (DS3)	44.736	672
T-4 (DS4)	274.176	4032

Wave-Division Multiplexing

Optical fibers absorb light energy differently at different wave lengths (colors). There are, however, wave lengths that are optimally conducting, and fiber transmission systems are designed to take advantage of the wave lengths where optical attenuation is minimum. It is possible, using certain fibers, to transmit two or more separate channels of information using different color light beams. This is called wave-division multiplexing (WDM). In essence, the different light beams are generated separately, merged onto the single fiber for transmission and separated at the receiving end. AT&T has introduced fiber-optic systems which multiplex up to 24,192 voice channels using framing techniques similar to those of the T-carrier hierarchy, and in some systems, WDM (Table 4).

Table 4
AT&T Fiber Systems and Capacities

System	DSX Framing	Year Introduced	Approximate Bit Rate	Voice-Circuit Capacity
FT3	DS3	1980	45 Mbps	672
FT3C	(2 DS3)	1983	90 Mbps	1,344
FTX-180	(4 DS3)	1984	180 Mbps	2,688
FT3C+FTX-180 (using WDM)	(6 DS3)	1984	270 Mbps (equiv.)	4,032
FT Series G 417	(9 DS3s)	1985	417 Mbps	6,048
FT Series G 417 (using WDM)	(18 DS3s)	1986	834 Mbps (equiv.)	12,096
FT Series G 1.7	(36 DS3s)	1987	1,668 Mbps	24,192

Summary

There are many more topics related to network and telecommunications technologies that have not been covered in this chapter, as well as many details that could have been added to the topics discussed. These are left to further investigation by the reader. The bibliography provides a wealth of additional sources for the interested reader. Nonetheless, the information that has been included should serve to provide at least the minimum necessary understanding of the field to facilitate further reading.

5

"Nothing is so difficult but that it may be found out by seeking."
(The Self-Tormentor) Publius Terentius Afer [190–159 B.C.]

Networks and Networking

Modern networks can be categorized into several general classifications, or network types. Categorization is often made based on geographic scope, function, switching techniques utilized, or other fundamental attributes of the network.

Wide-Area Networks (WANs)

Wide-area networks (WANs) serve geographically separate areas. These networks frequently link together metropolitan-area networks (MANs), discussed elsewhere in this chapter, thus enabling data terminals in one city to access data resources in another city or country. Intercity links are most frequently high-speed digital facilities (i.e., 56 Kbps or more) leased from interexchange common carriers.

Metropolitan-Area Networks (MANs)

Metropolitan-area networks (MANs) link together terminals, computers, etc., at many sites within a city area. Often the individual sites have their own local area network (LAN). Links between sites are frequently high-speed digital facilities leased from the local telephone company. MANs also frequently make use of bypass facilities, such as microwave radio or fiber-optic cable. Although much interest has been expressed in the past toward use of local cable-TV facilities to provide facilities for MANs, this market has not yet developed to any significant extent.

Local Area Networks (LANs)

Local area networks (LANs) are communications systems designed for local-site communications applications. LANs usually use coaxial cable as the transmission medium, however, some LANs use twisted-pair wire, optical fibers, radio, etc. They are usually high-speed, shared, data-communications networks. Integrated voice/data PBXs, or data PBXs (sometimes called data circuit switches, or DCSs) are also used for local data communications. Voice/data PBXs are typically used to switch both voice and data circuits, while data PBXs switch only data circuits.

41

Currently, applications requiring very high-speed data transfer are not accommodated well using the PBX. LANs have also found widespread application for factory-floor automation. The most popular application of LANs is to link together personal computers in office or other common work-group environments.

Switched Networks

Switched networks, as the name implies, are networks that utilize switching techniques. The most pervasive example of a switched network is the long-distance telephone network. Other switched networks include the local-access, or local exchange telephone network, as well as the numerous PBX installations with which the reader might be familiar.

Switched data networks are generally categorized as either transparent or transactional. Transparent networks, which use such switching techniques as circuit switching, polling, multiplexing, concentrating, etc., usually present the appearance to the user of being directly connected. Transactional networks, using such techniques as store-and-forward, message switching, or packet switching, usually appear to the user more like the postal system, wherein a message is addressed and sent to a specific recipient to be received at some later (albeit short) time.

Store-and-Forward Networks

A store-and-forward network operates in a manner which is nearly analogous to the postal system. The network processor assembles the message, and when the entire message is assembled, the processor packages it and sends it to the destination network switch where it is unpacked and sent to the end user. The collection, packaging, transmission, unpackaging, and subsequent delivery are performed by the network. Store-and-forward has existed for decades in telegraphy, where it is called message switching. Probably the most pervasive applications of store-and-forward networking in modern use are electronic mail, voice mail, telex and many radio paging systems.

Packet-Switching Networks

Packet switching is intended primarily for real-time machine-to-machine (i.e., nonvoice) traffic, including workstation-to-computer connections. A packet-switching network usually delivers its packet (i.e., message or part thereof) in a fraction of a second while a classical message-switching network often delivers its message in a fraction of an hour.

Packet-switching networks typically divide up long messages into manageable pieces that can be easily stored and transmitted rapidly from node to node. This provides the opportunity to send different parts of the longer message over different physical routes (although this is seldom done in existing systems), thus allowing the possibility of better facilities utilization. Since various parts of the message can be sent over different facilities, the security of the message content can also be improved.

Value-Added Networks (VANs)

Public packet-switched data networks (PDNs), as defined by CCITT Recommendation X.25, first emerged at the end of the 1970s. These so-called value-added networks (VANs) use computer-based technology to add value to the underlying facilities they typically lease from the common carriers. The emergence of VANs was, in part, due to user demand for access to information held on remote databases. Early PDNs included Packet Switch Stream (PSS) in the U.K., Transpac in France, Datapac in Canada, and Tymnet and Telenet in the United States. Over 100 countries have introduced or plan to install PDNs. Penetration of these services extends not only to the major industrialized nations, but also to Asia, Africa, and Latin America, and is probably a major factor in their increased popularity and use (e.g., with the exception of a very few direct dedicated private circuits to the U.K. and Canada, nearly all of the foreign traffic to OCLC is carried by one or more of the PDNs).

Several international standards are of interest regarding PDNs. CCITT Recommendation (i.e., the CCITT term for standard) X.25 defines the interface between a user's packet-mode terminal equipment called data terminal equipment, or DTE, and the packet network, whose entry point is known as the data circuit-terminating equipment, or DCE. Also of interest are the CCITT X.3/X.28/X.29 Recommendations. Since many terminals are not capable of handling the X.25 protocol (e.g., asynchronous character-oriented, or so-called dumb terminals), it is necessary to provide a device, called a packet assembler/disassembler, or PAD, to provide the necessary functions. X.3 defines the various PAD parameters. X.28 defines the terminal (DTE) to PAD protocol to be used, while X.29 defines the host PAD to terminal PAD protocol. Since it is often desirable for two or more PDNs to intercommunicate, CCITT has defined the X.75 Recommendation, which provides this functionality. User addressing, although necessary and important on a given packet network, becomes even more important when these networks interconnect. CCITT Recommendation X.121 describes an international numbering plan for PDNs.

Normally, devices using the switched telephone network for access to a PDN use asynchronous protocols. CCITT Recommendation X.32 defines how "X.25" terminals (e.g., personal computer workstations) gain access to PDNs over the dial network. X.32 provides for dial-in by the terminal (required), dial-out by the PDN node (optional), and secure dial-back by the PDN node (also optional). Secure dial-back is a security procedure whereby a user dials the PDN node to log on to the network, but is asked to hang-up and the network calls back using a predetermined telephone number. Most European networks plan to implement X.32, which has been available in France since early 1985. United States VANs have often not used the X.32 standard (e.g., Tymnet X.PC), although there is now movement toward the standard in the United States. An important advantage of X.32 is the inherent ability to establish several logical connections, or so-called virtual circuits, over the single physical dial-access connection. This takes on added importance in light of prospective cost increases for dial-access connections using the local telephone network.

Evolution toward integrated services digital network (ISDN), discussed elsewhere in this chapter, is a strategic aim of most of the world's telephone systems. It should be possible to internetwork between ISDN and PDNs. CCITT Recommendation X.31 provides for the support of packet-mode terminal equipment by an ISDN. There are, however, some problems with this solution. X.25 carries its signaling information (i.e., call setup, call termination, etc.) in band — that is, in the same channel as the user data, while ISDN employs out-of-band signaling. Therefore X.31 requires two control phases, one out-of-band, which first sets up the data channel, and one in-band dealing with X.25 virtual circuit signaling. In addition, X.25 uses a different data-link layer protocol (i.e., high-level data link control, or HDLC — also called LAP-B), while ISDN specifies a slightly different protocol, called LAP-D. X.25 packet networks are likely to undergo fundamental change in the coming years. X.32 will likely cause short- to medium-term growth, while X.31 will likely stir considerable debate. ISDN will likely provide the majority of packet services in the long run.

Virtual Private Networks (VPNs)

In the past, transmission has primarily been accomplished over either the public switched telephone network, or via private dedicated facilities. Each method has had its advantages and disadvantages. Use of the public network, for example, has offered efficiencies due to the shared use of the available transmission facilities on a broad scale, but often imposed restrictions, such as the lack of assured circuit availability and private numbering systems (e.g., the ability to dial companywide, across many locations, as an internal extension on a PBX). Dedicated networks, on the other hand, provide assured availability — at least within the bounds of the reliability of the facilities — and enable implementation of private numbering systems, but may not offer the efficiencies and economies available with the public networks. With the advent of modern computer-based switching equipment in the public networks, it is now possible to provide many of the advantages of a private network, while using the public shared network for actual transmission. Such networks, which appear to the user to be dedicated private networks but actually use the public shared network, are often called virtual private networks. These services are now offered by several of the major interexchange carriers (e.g., Software Defined Network service, or SDN offered by AT&T).

Tandem Networks

In telecommunications engineering, there are two basic types of connections to a switch: line-side connections, which refer to connection of user stations to the switch; and trunk-side connections, which refer to connections between switches. A tandem switch is used to provide switching of trunk connections. In a typical hierarchical network, access switches are used to provide trunk connections to a higher-level — often multilevel — tandem network that provides switching and transport at the trunk level between access switches. With the advent of high-speed digital transmission capability, T-carrier tandem networks have increased in popularity among large telecommunications users. Since the all-digital T-carrier facilities are easily multiplexed into smaller capacity circuits, it is possible for a large user to construct a T-carrier-based tandem network that is capable of dynamically switching and routing both data and digitized voice between various access switching devices (e.g., digital PBXs, packet switches, etc.). By combining both voice and data traffic onto the tandem network, and by using the switching and multiplexing capabilities of the various switching nodes on the tandem network, the large user can generate significant economies of scale and substantial cost savings. It is important to note that, unlike some other networking techniques, the tandem network provides facilities to the various access switches. Therefore, various forms of traffic can be transparently combined independently on the tandem network, each with its own protocols or other characteristics, while enabling the sharing of transmission facilities to generate economies of scale and reduction of resulting costs.

Integrated Services Digital Networks (ISDNs)

Integrated Services Digital Network (ISDN) is a network of telecommunication and bearer services that provides, in concept, for telecommunication services on the basis of OSI standards. It is founded on the idea of a global network with uniform services and universally compatible terminals. The prerequisite for ISDN is digitization of the analog telephone network, which will permit the integration of all communications services at rates up to 64 Kbps. ISDN will provide the technology for transparent transmission from terminal to terminal.

Basic access to ISDN provides two user-information channels, called "B" channels, each with a transmission rate of 64 Kbps over the two-wire subscriber line, plus a 16 Kbps signaling channel, called a "D" channel, separate from the user information channels. This is called the 2B+D, or Basic Rate Interface (BRI). A high-performance interface consisting of 23 B channels and a 64 Kbps D channel (i.e., 23B+D), called the Primary Rate Interface (PRI), is also specified. A common channel signaling system, the CCITT Signaling System Number 7 (SS#7), discussed elsewhere in this book, is employed. It should be noted that outside North America a 2.048 Mbps digital signal is frequently used in place of the 1.544 Mbps signal. In these countries, the PRI is 30B+D.

A second phase of ISDN is being planned to support switched wideband digitized video distribution, as well as near-instantaneous retrieval of massive amounts of data from remote databases. CCITT refers to this second-generation ISDN as broadband ISDN (B-ISDN). B-ISDN, with a planned digital channel rate of 135.168 Mbps, is not expected to be available until the mid-1990s at the earliest. B-ISDN, sometimes called wideband-ISDN, or W-ISDN, is still in the infancy of its planning by CCITT.

Data-Over-Voice (DOV)

Data-over-voice (DOV) multiplexors use a form of frequency division multiplexing (FDM) to enable ordinary twisted-pair local-loop telephone lines to simultaneously carry both full-duplex (i.e., two-way simultaneous) data and voice traffic. Simultaneous voice telephone and data terminal usage is an ISDN-like feature currently only widely available using DOV. Originally designed to handle local area data communications traffic in offices, etc., it is now being considered by many telephone companies for use with their packet-switched network offerings. DOV multiplexors typically add two carrier tones well above the 0–4 KHz voice-frequency band, one at 40 KHz and the other at 80 KHz, to carry data in two directions. Some newer units use somewhat higher frequencies (e.g., 50 KHz and 100 KHz). More than 100,000 channels of DOV have been installed in the United States.

Centrex and CO-LAN

Centrex is a telephone company, central-office-based service designed to provide many of the advantages of a customer-premises-based PBX. Likewise, a central-office-based LAN (CO-LAN) service has evolved as a substitute for premises-based local area networks, although the functionality of CO-LANs is more akin to premises-based data PBXs. Considerable debate is focused on the role of these services in serving as a migration step toward integrated services digital network (ISDN). At least four of the seven regional Bell holding companies (Nynex, Ameritech, BellSouth, and US West) are including Centrex testing in their initial ISDN field trials, and many believe that Centrex can and will be an appropriate solution for many metropolitan end users as a migration step to future ISDN-based services.

Network Access Technologies

In the post-Divestiture era, provision of access to interexchange networks has provided many opportunities as well as problems. In addition to the facilities and services provided by the local telephone companies, many other so-called first mile/last mile options have gained user attention. These are collectively known as bypass access technologies.

Digital Termination System (DTS)

Digital Termination System (DTS), a microwave-based access technology, broadcasts from a central local location to many low-cost receivers, usually located on the roofs of the various users' buildings. DTS provides the business user with a data transmission capacity necessary for large computer operations, rapid facsimile, videotex, video teleconferencing, and voice communication. It is particularly well suited for providing business communication services in large, congested urban areas (e.g., New York City). DTS is currently available in more than 20 major metropolitan areas. The equipment at the user site costs in the neighborhood of $10,000 and typically provides up to 1.5 Mbps of capacity to the user's location. Radio-packet techniques are typically employed to share the facility in an effective manner among a number of users. The number of users served depends upon system capacity and the specific traffic patterns and volumes of the various users. DTS may not be cost competitive for low-volume users, but can be attractive for high-speed, high-volume applications.

Cellular Radio

With a cellular-radio system, a geographic area is divided into cells with radio transmitters/receivers (transceivers) located at the center of each cell. In this way, a limited number of radio frequencies can be shared, with the frequencies being reused within the various cells, and the mobile user "handed off" when traveling from cell to cell. A central location is connected to each cell and manages handing off users from cell to cell, as well as connecting the various users to the local telephone network, or to interexchange carriers. The cost of cellular telephones has dropped from about $5,000 in the early 1980s, to about $1,500 in early 1987. In many major cities, the cost of a cellular telephone in early 1989, complete with antenna and installation, was less than $500. There are currently more than 180 cellular systems operating in the United States, with new systems being implemented at a rate of several each month. Pocket-sized, full-feature cellular phones weighing only a few ounces and selling in the neighborhood of $2,500 have recently been announced. The price for these units is expected to drop below $500 by 1992.

Although cellular-radio systems are primarily used for mobile radio-telephone applications, the technology can be used for nonmobile applications as well. Since these systems provide an analog voice channel, it is possible to modulate data on this channel (i.e., to use modem devices to transmit data). Unfortunately, the process of handing off traffic between cells, although virtually unnoticeable during voice conversations, can cause data errors to occur. Signal fading, reflections from buildings, and other noise on the channel can also cause problems. Therefore, where such errors are unacceptable, provision must be made to detect and correct (or retransmit) data containing errors. This is most often accomplished either in the modem itself, or in the terminal equipment, when it has sufficient intelligence. Error detecting and/or correcting protocols are often utilized.

Basic Exchange Telephone Radio (BETR)

Basic Exchange Telephone Radio (BETR) is a new service proposed by the FCC that recognizes the emerging role for radio in local telephone networks. BETR is intended to provide subscriber telephone service in rural areas where the cost of installing and maintaining conventional wire lines is high. This is frequently due to low population density or difficult terrain. One current commercial product consists of a modularly designed base station and a fixed subscriber station whose telephone unit includes an EIA RS-232-C data port capable of handling up to 9,600 bps. The unit is able to maintain four conversations over one 25 KHz channel (as compared with one conversation over a single cellular 30 KHz channel). The base station can support about 100 simultaneous subscribers, with a range of about 40 miles. Each of the 100 available voice circuits can be assigned on a demand basis to any subscriber station, making the system capable of supporting several times that number of users. The telephone company cost of the system is about $2,800 per subscriber line — a very attractive alternative in rural areas for installation of new circuits or replacement of aging telephone company plant to upgrade service to millions of party-line users. This is expected to be reduced to about $1,800 by 1990. BETR has obvious implications for both voice and data access to interexchange networks.

Packet Radio

Packet radio involves the transmission of data by radio networks interfaced to data devices or computers. Packet radio extends the technology of packet switching to the broadcast radio domain. The nodes in a packet-radio network typically consist of identical equipment and share a single channel on which all data and control information are interchanged. The channel is usually allocated by dynamic contention (e.g., CSMA/CD, discussed elsewhere in this chapter). In a packet-radio network, each node is a packet switch that plays an active role in the management of the network by storing, forwarding, and making routing decisions regarding data in the network. The nodes serve both as data sources and data relaying stations. A packet-radio network is therefore a collection of packet-switching nodes that communicate with one another over multiple hops via broadcast radio (i.e., where the signals are intended for reception by multiple stations). Packet-radio networks are an alternative to physical lines for providing short- to medium-range data communication. In 1984, The University of California Division of Library Automation (DLA) demonstrated an experimental library packet-radio system in conjunction with its MELVYL online catalog system. There are other examples of the use of radio in library applications — often involving online communications with bookmobiles — but these most often simply use so-called radio modems, and do not employ more generally accepted packet-radio techniques.

The capacity of a packet-radio network is limited by the available radio bandwidth allocated to the network. In general, a higher transmission rate results in more throughput. Since radio waves tend to be both refracted (i.e., bent) and reflected — particularly in urban areas; arriving signals may have reached a node by paths of different lengths, and hence may be displaced in time from one another (i.e., multipath distortion). When the relative delay is of the order of the duration of one bit, intersymbol interference results, which has a disastrous effect on the received-bit error rate. Multipath delays are often of the order of five microseconds, which corresponds to a maximum data rate of several hundred Kbps — well below the typical 1–100 Mbps range for modern LANs. Frequency-division multiplexing techniques, used to establish separate transmission channels, and multiplexing protocols, used to split the transmission over several channels, can be effectively used to increase overall throughput and apparent transmission speed, while respecting the data-transmission speed limits imposed by such multipath distortion. Scarcity of radio spectrum in many convenient radio bands, and federal restrictions on allocated bandwidth also can impose limits on network channel bandwidth, and hence throughput. The FCC has, however, proposed allocating frequencies in the 1,700–1,710 MHz band, on a shared basis for a private radio service that would make it easier and cheaper to move terminals around offices, opening the door to packet-radio LANs.

Packet-radio networks have generally been viewed as freestanding networks, rather than as access mechanisms to larger networks. There is no reason, however, why local packet-radio networks could not serve economically and effectively as access mechanisms to larger national/international networks. This might be accomplished with a local-network node serving as a gateway to such a larger network (e.g., the OCLC dedicated network), enabling an entire campus or metropolitan area to gain access to the network through a single access point — without the need and expense of numerous leased lines and modems. For example, this technology might prove particularly attractive to a multi-branch public or school library system, enabling intersite administrative networking, access to a local library system, etc., and also providing gateway capabilities to regional, national, or international networks.

Very Small Aperture Terminal (VSAT) Satellite Networks

Made possible by recent technological developments, very small aperture terminal (VSAT) satellite earthstations are low-cost, small diameter — usually less than six feet in diameter and sometimes as small as two feet — receive or transmit/receive satellite microwave units. A typical VSAT network consists of 500 to 1000 VSAT stations and a large central hub earthstation. Typical broadcast applications (i.e., one-way transmissions) include news wire service applications, remote paging services — where the paging message is transmitted to the local paging transmitter via the VSAT, etc. Interactive systems' transmissions (i.e., where VSATs transmit as well as receive) are physically between the VSAT station and the central hub station, although logically they may appear to be between VSATs. This is accomplished by switching and retransmission from the hub station. Some applications are one-way from the VSAT to a central hub. An example might be transmission of weather data from remote sensing stations to a central location. Often, the remote VSAT location serves as a data concentration point, supporting multiple terminals or other access channels and transmitting the consolidated data using the satellite.

VSAT earthstations typically cost a few thousand dollars (e.g. $6,000 to $20,000, depending upon performance, throughput, redundancy, etc.), while hub earthstations usually vary between $1 million to $2 million. Therefore, for economic reasons, a hub earthstation is usually shared among many VSATs, either in a single network, or possibly several independent VSAT networks. The limiting factor is the aggregate traffic volume at any time, and the total traffic capacity of the hub earthstation and switching equipment. Frequently, customer VSAT networks share the vendor hub earthstation, with terrestrial telecommunications facilities used to link the customer central site computer, etc., with the vendor hub location. Space-segment (i.e., satellite-channel) costs typically range from $30 to $150 per month per VSAT station, depending upon traffic. This is determined by the number of VSAT stations that can effectively share a given satellite channel, taking into consideration the traffic requirements of each earthstation (i.e., the more traffic, the fewer earthstations).

Local Area Data Transport (LADT)

Local area data transport (LADT) is based on the X.25 packet-switching protocol. With LADT, the local loop that provides telephone connections to the telephone company central office is used to send data at higher frequencies than the voice signal (i.e., data-over-voice, discussed elsewhere in this chapter). Data can be sent at rates ranging from 1200 to 9,600 bps between two points within a local access and transport area (LATA). InterLATA data communications are achieved by connecting two LADT networks through an interexchange packet-switching network via an X.75 interface. Enhancements under development are expected to increase the LADT's simultaneous data handling capability to beyond 9,600 bps. LADT is thought to be an evolutionary step toward ISDN in the longer term.

Network Architectures and Topologies

Architecture, when used in reference to telecommunications networks, is often a somewhat ambiguous term. Much like the architecture of a building, it is intended to convey the overall manner in which the network elements are put together. It encompasses more than simply what network node is connected to what other network nodes, also describing the control mechanisms, switching and routing philosophies, etc. Network topology, on the other hand, deals with physical or logical distribution and interconnection of the nodes themselves. It should be noted that some networks have different physical and logical topologies (i.e., the topology of the physical interconnections may differ from the logical topology used in control and routing procedures).

Several topologies deserve note; namely, fully interconnected, mesh, star, bus, ring and tree (Figure 3). A network is said to have a fully interconnected topology if each network node is directly connected to every other node — often an expensive and unwieldy proposition with any but the smallest networks. A mesh, or gridlike, topology has some nodes connected to many others, providing alternative paths across the network.

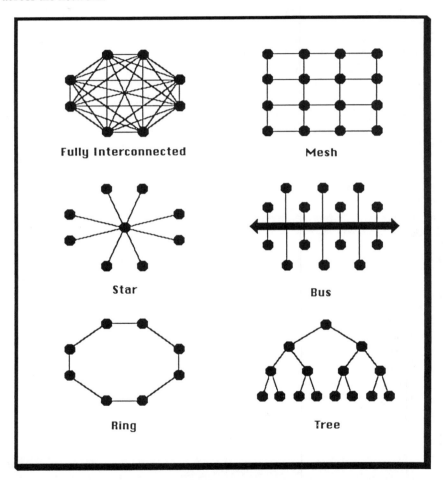

Figure 3 Network Topologies

In a star topology, a single hub location — usually a switch or computer — is connected to each node. The network elements then communicate through either physical or logical connections in the hub. The OCLC dedicated network is an example of a star network, with the various terminals communicating with the OCLC host computer complex or having messages routed to other terminals via the central hub computers (e.g., interlibrary loan messages). PBXs, whether voice, data, or voice/data are typically configured in a star topology.

In a bus topology, connected devices typically connect to (i.e., are not an integral element of) the communications channel. The physical channel is usually open ended, with data flowing outward in both directions from the transmitting station. Sometimes two physical channels constitute the physical bus channel. This architecture consists of a "head-end," an "inbound," and an "outbound" cable. The network station monitors the outbound cable and transmits on the inbound cable. The head-end monitors the inbound and retransmits the signals on the outbound cable. In some architectures, the head end may also perform other maintenance and control functions. The station can monitor and access the bus, but not physically intercept or block the bus; thus any signal on the channel is eventually seen by all monitoring stations, although at slightly displaced points in time due to propagation delays. This means that a station can be turned off, disconnected or unavailable for some other reason, and communications can still take place over the bus. The exception to this is in hierarchical network architectures where gateways, discussed elsewhere in this chapter, are interposed between network layers. When gateways are used, various subnetworks may not see all transmissions, and a gateway failure, obviously, could cause significant problems.

In a ring network, messages circulate in a loop, passing from station to station in bucket-brigade fashion. In the most common case, data flows in a single direction around the ring. Since the stations are an integral element of the network, the unavailability of a single network station can disrupt traffic flow over the network between stations that depend upon the missing station to relay their transmissions. The other side of the coin is that since various network segments are physically separate, it is possible — where the architecture permits — for several simultaneous transmissions to occur between various proximate stations. In larger networks, it is often quicker and easier to identify faults on a ring network, since only the segment between two identified stations need be examined.

In a tree topology, multiple branching connections are formed in a hierarchical arrangement. A station usually transmits to a higher level network node, which passes the message along to another station or to an even higher level network node. The diagram of such a network resembles a tree, with multiple layers of branching leading to the stations at the end.

The network architecture historically used in the long-distance telephone network in the United States was a five-level hierarchy, in which successively higher level offices, called classes, concentrated traffic from increasingly larger geographical areas. When a call was attempted, it entered the network at the lowest level. If the call could not be completed at that level, it was switched to the next higher level for further switching. This process proceeded until the call was completed, the highest level was reached, or it was determined that the call could not be completed (e.g., the station being called was in use or unknown, or the switch or trunk capacity for all possible routes was fully utilized, etc.). Although sometimes referred to as a tree, the historical long-distance network was not, in the strictest sense, a pure tree since peer switches could communicate directly without going through a higher level office. The similarity is, however, sufficient to convey the idea of how a tree network topology might work.

There are at least two important points to note regarding the preceding example:

1. The call is routed up and down through the hierarchy, which may not be the most expeditious route, with information concerning the status of the station being called or the status of subsequent intermediate switches or trunks remaining unknown until the point in time when the final disposition of the call is determined (i.e., the call is completed, or it is determined that the call cannot be completed).

2. The valuable intermediate trunk facilities, switch ports, etc., are dedicated to the incomplete call during this process, since it is these facilities that are in use to set up the call (i.e., in-band signaling).

Common Channel Signaling

An important aspect of currently emerging long-distance network architectures involves the common channel signaling (CCS) techniques that are being employed for network access and internal network operations. CCS techniques enable the interconnected networks, switches, and other network elements to easily communicate necessary information to enable provision of customer services and to accomplish network administration and maintenance functions. This means that an interconnecting data network (i.e., a packet-switched network in actual practice) can be used to quickly and efficiently determine the status of the station being called, as well as the status of any intermediate switches and trunks before any actual network resources are seized. This also enables the most effective route to be established for the call under dynamic circumstances. CCS, based on the CCITT Signaling System Number 7, or SS#7, will serve an increasingly important role with the advent of the integrated services digital network (ISDN), where these capabilities will increasingly encompass more user terminal equipment.

LAN Technologies and Attributes

In the current networking environment, local area networks have gained a significant level of attention and popularity. In this light, certain LAN-specific technologies and attributes are worthy of mention.

Categories of LANs

LANs are often categorized as proprietary, special purpose, or general purpose. Proprietary LANs, while often having the advantage of being highly optimized, tend to lock the user into one vendor's hardware and software. Special-purpose LANs typically exist to support specialized applications, such as connecting robot controllers and other devices in a real-time manufacturing environment. General-purpose LANs can usually support a variety of vendors' hardware and software.

The Institute of Electrical and Electronic Engineers (IEEE) 802 standard defines a contention bus, a token bus and a token ring LAN. Contention and tokens are discussed elsewhere in this chapter. These are the most common LAN configurations, or topologies. In addition, the American National Standards Institute ANSI X3T9.5 Committee is formulating a high-speed fiber-optic LAN standard known as fiber distributed data interface, or FDDI. The FDDI standard is derived from the IEEE 802.5 token ring protocol, and is a 100 Mbps token ring using an optical-fiber medium, where the IEEE 802.5 is a 4 Mbps general-purpose ring. The FDDI proposes a primary ring and a secondary ring. Stations are interconnected by point-to-point fiber-optic links over a maximum span of 2 km. The IEEE 802.x family of LAN standards is reviewed in Table 5.

Table 5
IEEE 802.x Standards

IEEE 802.1: *High Layer Interface (HILI) Standards.* Although not yet available, 802.1 will detail how the other 802.x standards relate to one another and to the ISO/OSI model.

IEEE 802.2: *Logical Link Control (LLC) Standard.* Defines the functions of the LLC sublayer. 802.2 is positioned above the remaining specifications (i.e., 802.3 through 802.6) that define media-access-control (MAC) and physical-layer functions. 802.2 defines both a connectionless and a connection-oriented service.

IEEE 802.3: *CSMA/CD Standard.* Defines the CSMA/CD protocol.

IEEE 802.4: *Token Bus Standard.* Defines the token-passing bus access method protocol.

IEEE 802.5: *Token Ring Standard.* Defines the token-ring access method protocol.

IEEE 802.6: *Metropolitan-Area Network (MAN) Standard.* Although not yet available, 802.6 applies to the MAC sublayer and physical-layer definitions for a metropolitan-area network using broadband transmission technologies.

Baseband vs. Broadband

Two common categories of LANs are baseband and broadband. Broadband LANs divide the capacity of the media (usually coaxial cable) using frequency division multiplexing (FDM). They operate in a manner analogous to cable television systems, transmitting several different channels using different frequencies. It is not uncommon for broadband LANs to share the media with other networks, for example other LANs, video distribution or teleconferencing applications, etc. Baseband LANs use some sort of time-division multiplexing (TDM) to share the capacity of the channel. Baseband LANs often use carrier sense multiple access with collision detection (CSMA/CD), or token techniques, discussed elsewhere in this chapter.

Access Control and Arbitration

When multiple stations communicate over the same channel, some method of ensuring that the separate communications do not interfere with one another is necessary. This is typically accomplished in one of two ways; namely, by ensuring that one and only one station has authority to transmit on the channel at any given time, or by allowing stations to transmit more-or-less at will, provided the channel appears to be idle, and providing for mechanisms to resolve any resulting contention.

Polled Networks

Some private networks (e.g., the OCLC dedicated network) approach this problem by assigning control of the network — or a portion thereof — to a computer (telecommunications processor). This is typically the case on multipoint leased-line networks. The processor addresses, or polls, each station to invite that station to transmit data on the channel. The priority process may be simply to poll each station in order, but more often this process is much more sophisticated, taking full advantage of the capability of the telecommunications processor. The processor may, for example, poll stations according to recent traffic activity, the priority of the application being used, the type of traffic transmitted by the station in the recent past (e.g., interactive, as compared to bulk data transfer), whether the station belongs to the company president or security officer, etc. Although not always the case, polled networks often restrict direct traffic flow to remote station-to-telecommunications processor communications. Even if this is the case, remote stations are sometimes allowed to communicate indirectly by means of the telecommunications processor (i.e., the message is passed along).

Token Networks

Specific access control is also frequently implemented using a so-called token. These networks, which include the IEEE 802.4 Token Bus and IEEE 802.5 Token Ring networks, establish a sequence of stations with the right to transmit, or token, being passed explicitly from one station to the next until the token returns to the initial station. The token itself is a uniquely identifiable data packet. In some schemes (e.g., IEEE 802.5) the token simply flows on the network, and a station wishing to transmit must capture the token. The token is then placed back on the network when the station has completed its transactions over the network.

CSMA/CD

The carrier sense multiple access with collision detection (CSMA/CD) access method is based on a contention mechanism. Any station on the network may attempt to initiate communication on the network at any time, provided the channel appears to be idle (i.e., no carrier signal is sensed at the remote-station location; an indication of traffic from another station). If traffic is present, the station simply defers its transmission until it senses the channel is idle. Unfortunately, collisions, which yield both communications unintelligible, can occur for at least two reasons:

1. Two stations can sense a clear channel and begin transmitting at the exact same time.

2. Propagation delays on a channel, or signal processing delays, may result in the situation where one station is already using the channel, but the signals simply haven't yet reached a second station wishing to seize the channel.

Collision detection schemes, such as the one used by IEEE 802.3 networks, require that a transmitting station monitor the channel to detect such a collision, cease transmission when a collision is detected, and then wait a random period of time before attempting to use the channel again. The reason for the random wait is to avoid a synchronizing of the two stations, a situation that would result in the two contending stations sensing an idle channel, transmitting at the same time, detecting the collision and aborting their transmission, waiting the same time period, mutually sensing a clear channel, transmitting at the same time, ad infinitum.

Slotted-Channel Techniques

Also worthy of note are slotted channel and reservation techniques sometimes used in contention systems. Because of propagation delay on the channel, particularly with satellite channels, the channel may appear idle to a station wishing to transmit, while elsewhere on the channel another station may already be transmitting. This can increase the chance of collisions on the channel. Some systems divide the channel into time slots. Although a time slot may present itself to different stations at slightly different points in time, the slots appear unique and distinguishable to each station, and hence reduce the probability of collisions on the channel. It should be noted that although the channel is divided in time, this is not a true form of time division multiplexing, since the slots are allocated by contention. A penalty for using slotted channel techniques is a level of added complexity in the stations.

Reservation Techniques

An even more sophisticated form of the slotted channel approach involves reservation techniques. Although there exist various techniques for accomplishing reservation, all operate by allowing a station to seize an unreserved channel slot and notify all other stations of its intent to use certain future channel slots that are still available. Thus, other stations know in advance that a particular slot will be in use. These techniques can result in a substantial reduction in chance collisions. The penalties involved are some element of increased overhead on the channel itself, and a considerable degree of increased complexity in the system.

Although basic contention systems seem to work well at low channel utilization, as traffic increases, so do collisions that result in the need to retransmit data. This can cause the actual channel throughput to decrease as a function of increasing demand, as well as network response times to increase. Slotting techniques increase the channel throughput, but at some increase in both complexity and response time on the network, since the transmitting station must wait for the beginning of the next available time slot. Reservation techniques increase throughput even further, but at the cost of even greater network response time and complexity.

User Experience

There is now emerging a body of user experience with LANs, and information about how users themselves rate the various LANs is now available. In a recent survey of over 600 users, these users were asked to rate their LANs in specific areas ranging from ease of installation to network performance under heavy load, and the interested reader is referred to the study itself [*Datapro*..., "Users Rate Their LANs."]. The ratings tend to indicate that users are generally pleased with both the performance of their LANs, and their LAN vendors.

Protocols and Protocol Issues

A communications protocol is, in its simplest terms, a predetermined and mutually agreed upon step-by-step procedure whereby the parties to a communication understand how the communication will begin, proceed, and end. In the field of telecommunications, many protocols have been developed and implemented. A number of protocols have been accepted as national and/or international standards. Several others, although not official standards, have been accepted through widespread and common usage — often supported by major computer equipment or telecommunications service providers.

Standard vs. Nonstandard Protocols

At first glance, it would seem that few reasons could be given for implementation of nonstandard protocols. There are many powerful justifications for use of standard protocols, and clearly many advantages can result from the use of standards. It should not be overlooked, however, that standard protocols result from the standards process, which by definition involves negotiation and inevitable compromise among various candidate standards or protocol elements — as well as the potential competitive position of the existing or planned products of the various suppliers who are frequently involved in the standards process.

It is sometimes possible to construct nonstandard protocols that are highly optimized to a specific application, or network environment. This can produce significant efficiencies or cost advantages, but must be balanced against the numerous disadvantages. An example in point might be the OCLC proprietary dedicated-network protocol. Although developed and implemented in the early 1970 time frame — before the adoption of most of the current network protocol standards — it continues to serve to the present time in a specialized network running specialized applications with an efficiency and cost-effectiveness which is uncommon in today's environment. To further make this point, effective average connect-hour costs, networkwide, on the dedicated OCLC private network in early 1989 were in the neighborhood of $1 per connect hour when the dedicated terminal is utilized in the neighborhood of 40 hours per week — about $1.36 per hour for typical usage patterns. This compares with typical VAN connect-hour costs which seldom drop below $5 per hour, and often range from $6 to $10 per hour or more, all charges included. This despite the rather large cost increases experienced by OCLC, in percentage terms, in recent years. This is not to minimize the impact of telecommunications cost increases on OCLC users, but should emphasize that under certain circumstances, nonstandard network protocols can result in significant optimization.

There is, however, a substantial price to be paid for lack of standardization in private networks. Again using the OCLC System as an example, proprietary protocols necessitate proprietary terminal products — terminals themselves, or at a minimum proprietary terminal software for microprocessor workstations. This has the effect of reducing the options and flexibility of the user, as well as the supplier, in many regards. The nonstandard nature of a network also lends a level of complexity and added costs in some cases, and may well render impossible in other cases, use of more standard local or regional networks for access to that network — something generally viewed as advantageous by user and supplier alike. More importantly, the highly optimized nature of the nonstandard network, geared toward the provision of a highly specialized service, or class of similar services, can prove highly disadvantageous as a supplier attempts to introduce and provide different services, or possibly the same services in a different manner. In general today, new network implementations — including new systems planned by OCLC — tend to evolve around accepted standards, although there has certainly not emerged unanimous agreement regarding just which standards will be universally used.

Open vs. Closed Systems

The terms "open" and "closed" system have been used (and too often abused) in a multitude of contexts with a multitude of intended meanings. They are mentioned here, if for no other reason, to emphasize the associated ambiguity. It is probably fair to state, however, that most generally the term open system is used to convey the concept of interoperability of various vendors' products or systems. Of course, the International Standards Organization (ISO) has an expanding suite of standard protocols associated with its Open System Interconnection (OSI) model, but too frequently vendors have described their proprietary architectures as being open, even when they may not have been compliant with these standards; therefore, "compliance" and "interoperability" rather than "open system" more succinctly get to the OSI issue.

The term "closed system" is sometimes used to convey the concept of a closed user group, or closed resource. For example, an online system where information is both exclusively provided by, and exclusively used by, a defined community of users may sometimes be called a closed system, regardless of the technical architecture of the system. In this context, an open system would connote the converse (e.g., an open-access, local online bulletin-board system).

Competing System Architectures

Many competing system architectures have gained, or are gaining, user acceptance, partly because of increased functionality and partly because of growth patterns or other affiliations. Too often these architectures are virtually incompatible. Examples include the IBM Systems Network Architecture (SNA), the Department of Defense Transmission Control Protocol/Internet Protocol (TCP/IP), and the ISO Open Systems Interconnection (OSI) architecture under which the Manufacturing Automation Protocol/Technical and Office Protocols (MAP/TOP), the Linked Systems Project (LSP) protocols, and other protocol suites have evolved or toward which they are moving.

OSI

OSI is a distributed systems architecture that is gaining international acceptance. In brief, the OSI reference model forms the basis for a series of standards aimed at allowing geographically distributed processes to implement an application cooperatively. These standards are intended to provide the facilities that allow application processes to communicate without regard for differences in hardware, operating systems or data representations. In the area of library and information science, the Linked Systems Project — a joint networking implementation involving the Library of Congress, OCLC, RLG, and others — is probably one of the leading examples of the use of OSI standard protocols, although as currently implemented, even the LSP is not strictly OSI compliant.

SNA

Systems Network Architecture (SNA) is the IBM proprietary communications architecture and protocols. Introduced by IBM in 1974, the structure of SNA is a layered architecture much like OSI. SNA does not, however, provide full scale support of the OSI protocols. Although IBM has indicated some level of commitment to the OSI protocol suite, movement in this direction has been slow, at least in the United States. More progress would appear to be in evidence outside the United States, particularly in Europe, but many of these advances are not yet available in the United States. There is reason to believe, however, that this may change in the future.

TCP/IP

Transmission Control Protocol/Internet Protocol (TCP/IP) is a protocol suite used extensively to provide a level of interoperability on the Defense Data Network (DDN), among other networks. With initial work having begun in the early 1970s, the TCP/IP protocols stabilized around 1980. TCP/IP enjoys a wide vendor support base and user population, particularly among major universities where military or related research is being, or has been, carried out. As of April 1986, the Department of Defense Advanced Research Projects Agency (ARPA) Internet, which is thought to be the largest unclassified TCP/IP internetwork, was estimated to have 2,400 host computers residing on 400 networks connected via 120 gateways, and was further believed to be growing at a rate of about 10% per month. Unfortunately, TCP/IP is not compliant with the emerging ISO-OSI protocol standards. This is particularly troublesome for the library and information science community that has generally strongly endorsed the OSI standards, and mechanisms to accommodate the widespread use of TCP/IP will clearly be necessary. Although the United States government has indicated its intent to migrate to the OSI standards, this will likely take some time. TCP/IP is expected to remain the most popular means of achieving multivendor communications over the next three to five years. The ISO-OSI protocol suite, however, is expected to overtake TCP/IP and eventually become the multivendor standard.

MAP and TOP

Manufacturing Automation Protocol (MAP), a factory-oriented set of specifications promoted by General Motors, is based on the IEEE 802.4 token-passing bus specifications. Technical and Office Protocols (TOP), an office-oriented set of specifications promoted by Boeing Computer Services, is based on the IEEE 802.3 CSMA/CD specifications. This recognizes the fact that token-bus and CSMA/CD networks are suited to different applications. In a factory network, a small delay per station can become less crucial than the guarantee that each station will have a chance to transmit before the one preceding it online gets to send a second message. To appreciate this, one has only to visualize an automated milling machine or robot welder blocked off the network by a verbose prior station. On the other hand, an office LAN might have many stations with relatively infrequent network requests, and since office workers are not likely to all submit their requests to the network at the same time, collisions might be tolerable.

MAP and TOP have identical structures in the higher layers of their definitions. Both use the IEEE 802.2 logical link control standard. They also share a common MAP/TOP Users Group. Probably the most significant aspect of MAP/TOP is the impact they have had on making available interoperable systems from various competing vendors — an indication of what user communities can accomplish when they put their commitment and support behind the effort for standardization.

Internetworking

An "internetwork" or "internet" is a network of interconnected computer networks. An internet can be used to combine (i.e., interconnect) heterogeneous individual networks. It can also serve to interconnect homogeneous networks, allowing different organizational areas control over their respective component network, while enabling intercommunications. The requirements to accomplish internetworking include: a consistent form of internet addressing — to enable communication between users on the various constituent subnetworks; points of interconnection between the networks; a mechanism to route and control the flow of information on the internet; and common protocols at some level — to enable different constituent networks to communicate with each other. The final requirement may, however, be eliminated by the use of gateways, which are discussed below.

Gateways, Bridges, and Relays

The concept of a gateway, bridge or relay connotes interconnection of different networks or systems. Often, however, the distinction between these terms is subtle or unclear. A gateway is a device which allows exchange of information between two dissimilar systems that require some type of protocol conversion. The term "bridge" is used with reference to the interconnection of networks that have a uniform address space, i.e., every station on the interconnected networks has a unique address. The bridge does not provide protocol conversion, but simply knows enough about the protocol to be able to perform some minor routing functions based on its knowledge of which network provides access to which address groups. A typical bridge application is the physical interconnection of similar local networks. A bridge application operates at a higher level than the so-called relay, which is merely used to extend the reach of a particular medium (e.g., a bus extender).

Intelligent Gateways

Although seldom, if ever, used in telecommunications or networking, the term "intelligent gateway" has arisen in the field of library and information science — and more recently, within the realm of telephone company provided access to information services. This term is usually applied to a computer application — often residing on a large mainframe computer — that provides user functions such as pre- and post-processing of information queries or responses, query or response translation, access to multiple information services through a single administrative account, directory or other database services, etc. Although intelligent gateways may provide certain legitimate gateway functions, they are distinguished as computer applications that provide user functions beyond those required simply to interconnect networks. It is interesting to note that the Bell operating companies were recently granted permission by the federal court overseeing the Divestiture agreement to engage to a limited extent in the provision of information gateway services, a form of intelligent gateways.

Encapsulation

Encapsulation is a technique sometimes used by two or more systems or networks to communicate using an intervening incompatible network. By encapsulating an internet packet of one type in the header of the intermediate network, the intermediate network can be used to connect these otherwise partitioned networks. In simple terms, the incompatible packet is hidden intact in the data portion of the intervening network packet as it passes between the end networks. This is sometimes called a hybrid network. If the technique is used to pass data both ways across the intervening network, it is called mutual encapsulation.

Internet Flow Control

Internet flow control is used to prevent the possibility of deadlock in the gateways and to provide graceful performance degradation when gateways are overloaded with internetwork traffic. A deadlock situation, sometimes called "deadly embrace," can arise when both parties to a communication find themselves in a condition requiring a response from the other party before they can proceed; hence no traffic can flow between the two parties while they wait for responses from each other — a curious, but fatal condition. Graceful degradation relates to the gradual worsening of performance on a network as traffic levels increase, rather than a sudden and catastrophic failure when some maximum traffic volume is encountered. There are numerous techniques designed to accomplish flow control, but they all share the characteristic of ensuring that more traffic is not placed onto the network than can be successfully processed and delivered.

LANs vs. PBXs

The advantages of bringing together voice and data traffic are apparent and have been discussed elsewhere in this book. Unfortunately, voice and data often provide very different characteristics and requirements. This is often inherent in the PBX and LAN systems, which have been designed primarily for voice and data traffic respectively.

Both PBXs and LANs are designed with the criteria of connectivity in mind. About one-third of the traffic on a typical PBX is outgoing to the telephone network, one-third incoming from the telephone network, and one-third is between stations on the PBX itself. Therefore, providing transparent connectivity over the telephone network is a primary objective with regard to the design of the PBX. LANs also are concerned with providing connectivity between stations on the LAN, but not as much concerned with transparent connection over the telephone network as with providing the perception of transparent connectivity between stations on the LAN.

Often due to the typically high level of exposure of PBX systems — both internal and external to an organization; availability is a major concern. Although availability is important with LANs, the degree of backup and support typical in PBX systems is often not present in LANs, primarily because of the way LANs are typically used.

Throughput capability is frequently of significant importance to LANs. Throughput from the perspective of a LAN relates primarily to the aggregate amount of data the LAN is capable of transporting without significant degradation of response time. Throughput, from the perspective of the PBX, relates more to the number of simultaneous connections that can be made between PBX stations and the outside telephone network, or among one another, than to the amount of aggregate data the PBX is capable of handling.

Quality of transport is often of significantly more importance to LANs (i.e., bit-error rate) than in the voice applications, where understandability is more the objective. Real-time operation is also of significant importance for PBXs. Any noticeable delay in transmission is particularly annoying for voice communications, while often well tolerated with data transmissions over LANs. Speed, from the point of view of a PBX, often means how quickly a call can be placed, while speed is more often related to bandpass (i.e., data rate) from the perspective of the LAN.

Current PBX technology easily provides for a 64 Kbps digital channel between data terminals on the PBX. Cost appears to have emerged, however, as a major potential disadvantage of the use of circuit-switching PBXs for data, although this is a subject of some debate — particularly when operating and support costs are taken into consideration. While LANs optimize the utilization of the transmission medium and attempt to minimize the cost of connection — typically a higher cost for PBXs — the shared nature of the transmission medium and the dynamic bandwidth allocation typical of LANs can introduce delays which can readily become unacceptable for voice traffic. This is particularly true as loads increase on the LAN. For these reasons, it would appear that, for the present at least, optimizing voice and data transmissions imposes divergent demands on design priorities. Movement toward integration of voice and data however, is clearly present — as hinted by the emergence of much activity related to ISDN.

Fiber Optics vs. Satellites

Fiber-optic systems are evolving at an almost astounding rate. Fiber typically provides more capacity and capability for less money, and the availability of fiber is increasing dramatically. This being the case, the future would appear to look dim for satellites — and in fact it is not nearly so bright today as it was just a few years ago. A combination of the technical and economic advantages typically associated with fiber, and the problems of the space industry of late, which have caused rising insurance rates and delays in satellite launches, do not bode well for satellites.

Although, in the view of the author, fiber-optic systems are the rising stars of the telecommunications transmission world, there will likely be a place for satellites for at least the intermediate term. It will be some time until fiber penetrates ubiquitously to remote areas, even though a national backbone fiber network has already evolved. Very small aperture terminal (VSAT) applications of satellite technology will offer an attractive option for users where access costs to major fiber networks are high, or access is simply not yet available. Elsewhere in the world, it may also be some time before fiber networks become pervasive, although this will likely be sooner than many suspect. Hence, satellites will remain a viable and economic transmission technology. Satellites are expected to continue to lose dominance to fiber-optic systems, but there will remain a place for communications satellites for at least the coming five to ten years, and most likely much longer.

Premises Wiring Issues

Premises wiring is the cable, equipment, etc., associated with providing telecommunications connections between telephones, computers, PBXs, etc., within a specific building or complex. Traditionally, premises wiring has been based on twisted-pair wire connecting telephones with a PBX, or the telephone room where Centrex connections were made. This often involved provision for connecting to convenient cross-connect blocks (i.e., devices for connecting local wire to the central system), often located on each floor of the building, and providing appropriate cabling between the cross-connects and the central telephone room. This also included necessary administration and tracking of the inventory of wire connections in the system — although unfortunately, this is an often neglected function in the experience of the author. With the advent of data terminal equipment throughout the premises, LANs of different types began appearing in different work units or departments, etc. Provision of premises wiring has since taken on a new and more complex dimension, and unfortunately, many building cable troughs have become hopelessly congested.

Fortunately, a standard architecture for premises wiring systems has been endorsed by several major corporations, including IBM, AT&T, DEC, and Hewlett-Packard. The architecture consists of three main components:

- Horizontal wiring, which is preinstalled twisted-pair cables that run between wall outlets in each work area and the wiring closets

- Wiring closets, which are both termination points for the drop cables in the horizontal wiring and an administration point where the user can perform interconnection and patching to the backbone

- Backbone wiring, which is used for interconnections between wiring closets

Wiring closets provide the opportunity to install fiber-optic equipment for use on the backbone.

Such a scheme may address the needs of a central PBX or Centrex system, and may even begin to address the needs of twisted-pair-based LANs, but unfortunately, does little to address the need for coaxial-cable-based LAN networks. It would appear to the author that premises wiring will remain a potential problem area, at least until the arrival of ISDN. About the best advice that can be offered in the interim is careful planning and detailed administration of premises wiring facilities. It should also be noted that numerous ownership and regulatory issues have recently emerged with regard to inside wire, and these are discussed in more detail elsewhere in this book.

Network Management

Ongoing operation of networks requires careful monitoring, traffic analysis and forecasting, and diagnostic capabilities. This is the function of network management. Unfortunately, most existing network management systems are proprietary in nature. Each vendor computer system that is added to the network has its own network management system, even though the equipment included in, or attached to a network may be fully X.25 compatible. While the International Standards Organization (ISO) has been successful in establishing the open systems concept for data-path standards, it has not yet agreed on the protocol structure for the management information. This means that not only is it necessary for network staff to learn to use several different systems, but also it is difficult, if not impossible, to correlate the data from the separate systems. The marketplace is, however, beginning to respond to this need. Many companies, among them Avant-Garde, US West and Network Management Inc., are announcing vendor-independent network management products. The announcement by IBM of its NetView and NetView/PC products represents an important strategic move that positions IBM systems as a potential umbrella under which multivendor support can develop. Given the scope of IBM in the marketplace, these products are likely to become de facto standards from which many new network management products will evolve.

Network Monitors

Network monitors provide a wealth of information to network developers and system managers; silent sentinels connected to the network watching over all activity. Some monitors are designed to capture all messages transmitted on the network, regardless of their origin or intended destination. This can allow their users to ascertain passwords, as well as other potentially confidential information on the network. Use of such a system at the Princeton University Computing Center, however, has led to the observation that the sheer volume of traffic transmitted over a busy network is sufficient to lend some amount of security to the system. Nonetheless, this is something of which users of networks should be aware.

Artificial Intelligence

The application of artificial intelligence techniques in the form of expert systems to telecommunications network management is likely to emerge as an important new area. Techniques described by AT&T in the context of fault-tolerant expert switching systems include error detection, error correction, system reconfiguration, automatic system reinitialization, and provision of system integrity under all operating and fault situations. AT&T Bell Laboratories has also developed an expert system for assisting in local loop maintenance.

Summary

Networks and networking technology, and more importantly, their application to the field of library and information science are evolving at a staggering rate. It is incumbent on the practicing professional in the field to stay abreast of these developments, and it is hoped that the fundamentals that have been presented in this chapter might play at least a small role in easing this burden.

6

"To predict the broad developments of the future is no more a
tour de force than to divine those of the past...If past events
have left their traces, it is reasonable to imagine
that those still to come have their roots."
Honore de Balzac [1790–1850]

The Telecommunications Infrastructure

This chapter reviews the telecommunications environment and infrastructure, discusses the major forces influencing change within this environment, and suggests certain likely outcomes, as seen by the author, that will have significant influences on the future telecommunications infrastructure. This information is then used as the basis in assessing likely impacts on various aspects of library and information systems, their providers, and users. Specifically discussed are impacts foreseen for:

- National online information providers

- Local online information providers

- Local and long-distance telephone companies as providers of information

- Users of information

Spheres of Influence

There are numerous influences currently impacting the area of telecommunications. These can be generally categorized into four major spheres:

1. Technology

2. Economics

3. Politics

4. Government (i.e., legislation, adjudication, and regulation)

Technology
The sphere of technology, as it impacts telecommunications, is probably the simplest to understand and to use as a basis for predicting likely future developments. The general areas most directly impacted by technology are:

1.   Transmission

2.   Switching

In the area of transmission, the advent of fiber-optic systems has revolutionized thinking with regard to transmission capacity, media size, and costs. This presents several revolutionary consequences. Optical transmission is most effectively accomplished using all-digital techniques, in contradistinction to the inherently analog techniques most common to other transmission technologies. This has significant implications for integration of heretofore distinct classes of transmissions (e.g., voice, data, video, etc.), with improved utilization of the facilities and greater economies of scale.

Another important inherent characteristic of optical-fiber systems is their potentially unlimited capacity in practical terms — estimated to be several thousand times greater than the fastest systems currently in operation (including currently installed fiber-optic systems). The enormous inherent capacity, combined with the significantly reduced physical size and cost and the inherent imperviousness to interference, corrosion, fire, and unauthorized interception of transmissions, make the technology extremely attractive. Optical fiber runs between $0.50 and $1.50 per fiber-meter in early 1989, and is expected to drop to a few cents per meter within three to four years. This has rendered the major costs of implementation those of securing rights-of-way and physical installation of the media, as compared with the cost of the media itself. This is not the case with other media — particularly when viewed in terms of cost per unit of capacity. For these reasons, tremendous inherent system capacity is currently being installed, where in the past implementation was geared to short- to medium-term capacity needs.

Satellite transmission technology has presented both opportunities and inherent disadvantages. Advantages include distance independence and relatively high capacity, particularly when compared with more common terrestrial transmission technologies such as local twisted-pair wire. The disadvantages include its inherent analog nature, signal delays due to the distances involved and the finite propagation velocity of electromagnetic radiation, cost — particularly compared with terrestrial fiber, and the inherent vulnerability of the satellite media to interception and interference.

Satellite capacity must be recognized as an expendable resource, having a finite life span typically determined by onboard fuel supply. Satellite technology represents, however, an attractive and viable alternative in the intermediate time frame — until other terrestrial technologies such as fiber optics achieve a more dominant position — and in the longer term, as a complementary technology in certain circumstances such as:

1.   Remote locations where newer terrestrial technologies may not be expected to penetrate for the foreseeable future

2.   Where local access costs to other media are unusually high

3.   Where access facilities provide unacceptable technical limitations

Very small aperture terminal (VSAT) satellite earthstations (i.e., typically less than two meters in diameter) can be expected to provide an attractive alternative in such regions, when data rates are not excessive.

Switching technology has evolved from a primarily electromechanical physical connection, through computer-controlled electronic physical connection, to a totally digital computer-based connection technology. This has reduced both switch size and cost as computer technology has evolved, dramatically improved capability and capacity, and is expected to continue this trend for the foreseeable future. In addition, the inherent digital nature of the modern switch presents a synergy with the digital nature of optical transmission media. This synergy is a driving force behind the emerging integrated services digital network (ISDN), which is discussed elsewhere in this book.

Economics

Within the sphere of economics, technology has driven the cost of both long-haul transmission and switching down dramatically. Recent developments in the area of satellite "space segments" (i.e., satellite links between earthstations) have somewhat tarnished the outlook for continued reduction in space-segment costs. The advent of fiber-optic technology has resulted in some reluctance toward investment in satellite technology. This, combined with the expendable nature of the asset due to limited onboard fuel supplies, the comparatively high risks associated with launch and operation of satellites, and related insurance rates exceeding 30% of launch value in early 1989, will result in the erosion of dominance of satellite space segment compared with terrestrial transmission as the most available, economic and attractive transmission media. Although primarily an economic issue, this shift is predominantly driven by technical factors.

Economics, which will play the predominant role in shaping the future of the telecommunications environment, are inextricably interwoven with technology and regulation. The impact of regulatory change will be a major force acting on the economic elements fundamental to the industry. It is important to note that these economic elements result from the interplay of several closely related but quite separate facets of regulation and regulatory change. Worthy of note is the shift from a situation where certain telecommunications services have historically been offered by the carriers at rates below the cost to provide these services, to a more cost-based structure. Instrumental in this process has been the separation of long-distance carriers from local telephone service providers as a result of Divestiture. This cost difference has historically been supported by cross-subsidization from other more lucrative services. An example is local service being subsidized by long-distance services.

Allocation of costs by various regulatory agencies has also resulted in anomalies in price structures. Noteworthy among these is the regulatory allocation of equipment costs between usage-sensitive elements and fixed-cost elements, and further regulatory allocation of these costs between local and long-distance services, and by state and federal jurisdiction (i.e., separations procedures). The practice of averaging certain costs on national or regional bases has also had a significant impact on rates.

Still another important economic aspect being significantly impacted by regulatory change is the depreciation of a large equipment base. Historically, both state and federal regulation dictated relatively long depreciation schedules for this equipment — based for the most part on physical life expectancy. This has had a twofold result:

1. Depreciation charges used by the regulators to determine subscriber rates were smaller than would otherwise result from more common depreciation methods and schedules, and hence resulted in lower subscriber telephone rates.

2. Since the physical rather than "useful" life of the equipment was the basis for depreciation, much of the equipment tended to become obsolete and noncompetitive in comparison with that of the evolving competitive providers.

With the advent of more competition in the industry, most regulators have recognized the need to move toward less conservative depreciation mechanisms and schedules, but unfortunately the various federal and state regulatory jurisdictions have not moved in a common direction with regard to either methodology or schedule. The reduction of this accumulated depreciation cost surplus (i.e., the excess of book value over actual value), which has been taken into the subscriber rate base, has nonetheless resulted in higher rates. In addition, accelerated depreciation schedules and ongoing modernization of the network will continue to increase rates in the future. This is true not only because of additional new capital investment due to modernization, but also because replacement of under-depreciated current equipment will result in additional write-offs.

Also not to be ignored is a recognition by federal legislators, particularly those legislators dealing with trade policies and commerce, that timely access to technical information is necessary if the United States is to be highly competitive in a world economy. This has been translated into federal efforts which are expected to promote deregulation and competition within the telecommunications industry, and provide impetus and support for the networks and networking activity necessary to achieve these objectives.

Politics

It is impossible to discuss regulation without a recognition of the realities of the American political system. Although many regulatory bodies are not elected, nonetheless they are usually responsive to an elected legislative body. The political realities are that elected officials are understandably sensitive to the need for reelection. This concern is typically focused toward at least two distinct audiences:

1. The respective voter constituency, whose votes are needed to remain in office

2. Special interest groups, whose financial and other support is necessary to the reelection process.

The legislator, and hence the regulator, must walk a fine line between these two audiences.

In the final analysis, however, it is the voter that often prevails when the two groups come into conflict, since the legislator is usually quick to realize that a disenchanted electorate is not conducive to reelection. This political reality is in the forefront of the debate and furor over rapidly rising residential telephone rates in the recent past — which interestingly, plays a major role in many of the broader issues confronting telecommunications regulators in the current environment. This is particularly relevant in light of the fact that local subscriber rates are substantially subsidized by long-distance and other services primarily supported by the business community — services also often economically available from competing sources.

Regulators thus find themselves on the horns of a dilemma. On the one hand, if they allow local service rates to rapidly move toward cost, the increased local rates will create a serious political problem. On the other hand, if they regulate local rates below cost, the carrier is forced to recover the shortfall from business customers, making it economically attractive for customers to bypass the local carrier completely. This further reduces the revenue base of the carrier and forces local subscriber rates up in order to recover the fixed cost of the local network — the very thing the regulators were attempting to avoid. The regulators cannot allow the carrier to incur sustained and massive losses, and government subsidies are not palatable in today's environment. It is this dilemma that has given rise to the "new social contract," a regulatory concept discussed later, and other plans for alternative regulatory mechanisms within the various states.

Legislation, Adjudication, and Regulation

The telecommunications industry is subject, as is all industry, to legislative control. This control has generally taken three forms:

1. Revenue collection

2. Antitrust

3. Regulation as a "natural monopoly" and an instrument of public policy

The last two concepts are fundamentally in conflict. Over the years, this incongruity has pitted the U.S. Department of Justice against AT&T in the courts, and brought the courts and the FCC into conflict as the courts have, in essence, entered into the regulatory domain through the mechanism of the Modified Final Judgment (MFJ), or Divestiture agreement.

It is important to recognize the relationships between the Congress that passes legislation and creates regulatory agencies, such as the FCC, to carry out delegated rulemaking; the Executive which is charged with enforcing the laws of Congress and the regulatory agencies; and the Courts where the inevitable conflicts are adjudicated. Understanding the intimacies of these relationships can be a key to predicting the future direction of many developments in the telecommunications environment.

Legal Separations and Jurisdictions

Telecommunications regulation falls under the jurisdiction of the several states, except to the extent that the "ether" — the boundaries of which are not confined within any state, and the use of which is governed by international treaty — or interstate commerce are involved. Thus, use of radio, microwave, satellite, etc., and communications which cross state or international borders fall under the jurisdiction of the Federal Communications Commission. All other aspects of telecommunications regulation fall under the jurisdiction of the several states or their respective regulatory agencies.

Further, the federal court, under the MFJ, has defined distinct regions called local access and transport areas (LATAs), which may or may not be contained within a single state jurisdiction. The MFJ provides that communications within a given LATA are provided by local exchange carriers (LECs), while communications between LATAs are provided by interexchange carriers (IXCs). An example of a LEC is the Ohio Bell Telephone Co. (that also happens to be a Bell operating company, or BOC—i.e., BOCs are LECs, but not all LECs are BOCs), while AT&T and MCI are IXCs. Communications between states, whether between LATAs or within a multistate LATA are subject to federal regulation. Since the LECs are prohibited by the MFJ from providing interLATA (i.e., long-distance) service, the potential for cross-subsidy between long-distance service and local-exchange service is minimized.

Further complicating the picture is the fact that defining what constitutes interstate communications, and particularly what constitutes equipment or activities related and necessary to interstate communications, is prone to uncertainty and difference of opinion. For example, it is necessary to install local-loop facilities to connect the subscriber's telephone to the local central office, whether or not the subscriber makes any long-distance calls. How the cost of the local loop should be divided between interstate and intrastate jurisdictions can be a subjective issue. These issues are the subjects of ongoing disputes, generally in the courts, between federal and state regulatory agencies, and often between the various carriers and both federal and state regulatory agencies, or sometimes even between the carriers themselves. This is so often the case that the FCC has created Federal-State Joint Boards, composed of FCC commissioners, state commissioners and limited staff, to help resolve such issues.

In addition to legal and jurisdictional separations within the regulatory process, there are also highly complex accounting rules which result in certain economic separations. These rules pertain primarily to the arbitrary assignment of costs between state and federal jurisdictions and between fixed (so-called nontraffic sensitive, or NTS costs) and usage or traffic-sensitive costs. The allocation of these costs is important in a regulated environment, since these cost allocations represent the basis from which subscriber rates are determined.

In the case of interstate communications, the FCC determines allocation of costs between the interstate and local exchange carriers. The commission further determines allocation of these costs between NTS and traffic-sensitive components. In addition, the commission prescribes certain mechanisms for recovery of these costs by the carriers. The state commissions do likewise for intrastate communications, except to the extent the FCC has preempted the jurisdictional authority of the state commissions.

There are at least three general concepts which are helpful in understanding the application of certain jurisdictional separations:

1. Preemption

2. Contamination

3. Intent

The principle of preemption (federal supremacy) has been established by the FCC through precedent, and asserts that the FCC can rule certain aspects or elements are related to interstate communications, and hence are subject to regulation by the FCC. The principle of preemption has, however, recently been called into question by a decision of the United States Supreme Court. When elements of a telecommunications system are used for both intrastate and interstate communications — albeit at different points in time — these elements, to the extent they cannot be separated, are generally considered to be contaminated and subject to regulation by the FCC. Costs related to these elements are often called joint access costs. Also, if the intent of a communication involves crossing a state boundary, then related facilities and equipment are subject to federal regulation. This is true even though the various transmission facilities may not be directly connected, and may reside within the boundaries of a single state. A classic example is a data network consisting of private leased telecommunications lines connecting several computers in different states, at least two of which reside within a single state. Under these conditions, the private line which connects the two computers located within a single state is solely subject to federal regulation if the communications it carries are routinely intended to be passed along to a computer in another state; hence, the intent of the communications is interstate, and the interposed computer is merely an incidental switch. It should be noted, however, that as the manuscript for this book is being completed, an FCC Federal-State Joint Board has proposed to put restrictions on the contamination doctrine, calling for facilities with less than a certain amount of interstate traffic (suggested to be less than 10%) to fall under state jurisdiction.

Pricing Principles

As the telecommunications industry has evolved from a highly regulated monopoly toward a more competitive market-based environment, pricing principles and strategies have changed, and continue to do so. Of the various pricing principles and strategies that have surfaced over the course of time, three are particularly worthy of note. These have often been referred to as:

1. Value-based pricing

2. Cost-based pricing

3. Strategic (market-based) pricing

Value-based Pricing

In a highly regulated environment, prices were fixed by regulatory bodies to reflect what was considered to be a reasonable and acceptable level for the services rendered. This value-based pricing strategy was not necessarily reflective of specific costs related to the provision of specific services, but in the aggregate was targeted by the regulators to enable recovery of the accumulated costs of the carrier with a reasonable return on investment for the carrier's stockholders. In some instances, prices were established with the objective of promoting public policy.

The value-based pricing strategy had several important and interesting aspects. First, as noted, the carrier's cost to provide a given service was not necessarily directly related to the price for that service. Second, value-based pricing often resulted in averaging of certain costs by the several carriers on a regional or national basis, depending upon service and regulatory jurisdiction. For example, the National Exchange Carriers Association (NECA) nontraffic sensitive (NTS) pool resulted in contributions of NTS related revenues by all carriers to a monetary pool. The pool was then allocated nationally on the basis of designated fixed costs required by each carrier to provide local service (i.e., the FCC attempted to remove accidents of geography and terrain from the provision of local service). An analogy might be to create a monetary pool consisting of mandatory contributions from local heating fuel providers on a national basis, and reallocating the funds on a state-by-state basis depending upon the average winter temperatures experienced by each state.

Third, value-based pricing tended to send inaccurate messages to consumers regarding specific services, and in general often tended to promote inefficient use of facilities and resources. An example of this phenomenon was the pricing of certain private-line services (e.g., multidrop private lines) below the established cost to provide these services. This resulted in organizations such as OCLC, and many others, building their network strategies on the basis of these comparatively inexpensive facilities (so-called tariff niche strategies), only to be very unpleasantly surprised when the facilities were later priced to more nearly reflect their actual cost. Additionally, value-based pricing, by its very nature, required that certain services be priced above their cost, in order to generate the cross-subsidies required by services which were priced below cost. The regulators tended to overprice services that were perceived as luxury services, or services primarily used by large business that could pass the costs indirectly to their customers.

Putting aside the issue of efficient use of resources, the system of value-based pricing worked reasonably well until the monolithic regulated monopoly approach to dealing with the industry began to be broached with the introduction of elements of competition in the provision of these services. It is also important to note that value-based pricing — as implemented by regulation — segmented the market by product or service alone, and not by customer, or customer class. With the first advent of competition, the delicate equilibrium necessarily required by value-based pricing was irreversibly upset. Competitors with different, and often more favorable cost structures — frequently due to selective market participation, and without the requirement to generate certain cross-subsidies — were put at an advantage over the established carriers. It was only a matter of time before the recognition of this incontrovertible fact by regulators and the industry alike, resulted in adjustments to the strategy by regulators in the early stages, with essential abandonment of the principle of value-based pricing with the advent of rampant competition and Divestiture.

Cost-based Pricing

With the advent of competition, and with the divestiture of the Bell system, it was recognized that the system of value-based prices could no longer be preserved. Since the major cross-subsidies had historically taken place between long-distance service and local exchange service, with long-distance service providing substantial elements of support for local service, the FCC moved toward establishing a cost-based pricing structure wherein each service would be priced to at least recover the cost to provide that service. It was soon recognized that the sudden shift to total cost recovery for local service was not politically attractive, and probably not politically achievable. With this realization, the FCC moved toward a more gradual approach to cost-based pricing, wherein certain subsidies would continue to be provided to local carriers from revenues generated by interexchange carriers.

In the absence of a clean cut from value-based to cost-based pricing, the FCC was in essence faced with the worst of both worlds. While they had reduced the threshold of pain produced by increasing local subscriber rates, they had far from eliminated it, and were faced with a continuing assault on all fronts with regard to this issue. On the other hand, they had not eliminated the necessity for subsidies, or the subsidies themselves. They were faced with reshaping, and in fact augmenting, the massive body of procedures and mechanisms for collecting, accounting for, allocating, and disbursing these subsidies among an ever more vocal and increasing number of carrier entities. To complicate matters even further, the FCC found it difficult, if not impossible to carry out a two-pronged policy of increasing competition within the industry and allowing market forces to come to bear, while at the same time providing effective and consistent mechanisms to collect the required subsidies from a myriad of new market entrants in an ever more dynamic technologically evolving environment. To add to the complexities of the situation, the FCC is empowered to regulate, and is specifically prohibited from imposing taxes, which has further restricted its ability to come to grips with the issue of collecting these subsidies.

Beyond the FCC, similar problems confront the several state regulatory agencies. It is not surprising that "Murphy's Law" has prevailed, and the several states have often chosen disparate approaches to the problems with respect to other states and the federal agency. To further complicate matters, in some instances the rules imposed by the states have been mutually inconsistent and are irreconcilable with federally mandated provisions, which has resulted in considerable controversy, not to mention a healthy portion of litigation between state and federal regulators.

The bottom line is that, in theory, cost-based pricing should provide a simple, satisfactory, and easily implemented solution to the problem. The hard truth is that, in practice, it has not been possible to implement. Further, the prospects for success in implementing pervasive cost-based pricing in the near term are optimistically placed at slightly above zero. The legislators, regulators, executive and judicial, at both the state and federal level, and most importantly the carriers, providers and users alike, would appear to be faced with a completely unsatisfactory situation from the perspectives of all concerned — although there are many different perspectives. Out of the morass appears to be materializing a possible solution for all concerned. Although it has been called by several names, and has not yet completely solidified, it seems to be most frequently referred to as strategic pricing.

Strategic Pricing

Regulators, particularly certain state regulators, have recognized that were it not for the backlash created by certain immediate consequences of cost-based pricing — most notably rapidly increasing local telephone rates — it would be an appropriate and acceptable solution to the problem. The increases in local rates necessary to cover costs are not necessarily in and of themselves a serious problem. When compared with comparable service in some other countries, or in terms of the price consumers are willing to pay for other services, these rates would not appear to be greatly out of line. The problem generally is subscriber expectations regarding the value of the service as a result of the message that has been sent with subsidized pricing over many years, and the rate at which the changes have been attempted.

The perceived solution is to provide certain safeguards in the short to intermediate term, where particular sensitivities are perceived to exist — particularly where these can be expected to produce adverse political ramifications. It is also necessary to recognize that cost-based pricing, in and of itself, is a regulatory concept. In a free market environment competition forces prices to marginal values based upon cost. Therefore, prices should tend toward marginal costs as regulatory intervention is reduced, if:

1. Steps are taken to control the rate of rise of prices for certain services where particular sensitivity to rapid increase has been identified

2. Certain elements that will help enable the subscriber to control to some degree the expenditure for these services in the longer term are employed

3. Competitive forces are assured in unprotected (i.e., unregulated) areas

The problem is how to realistically achieve items (1) through (3).

Achieving the situation described above is much more of a political problem than a regulatory one. The problem is to convince the interested parties that their various interests will be served. The political solution that seems to be evolving is focused under what is being most often called the new social contract. Under this approach the regulated carriers are offered the prospect of complete deregulation — usually by specific service segment — in return for temporary guarantees of service availability and price containment of the sensitive service costs according to prescribed limits and schedules. The old contract, of course, was provided by the Communications Act of 1934 through the concept of universal service at affordable rates in a totally regulated environment.

> *To make available, so far as possible, to all the people of the United States a rapid, efficient, nationwide and worldwide wire and radio communications service and adequate facilities at reasonable charges. [47 U.S.C. 151-609 (1976)]*

The strategic pricing element results from the flexibility given to the carriers to pick and choose how they will recover subsidies to meet the cost/price differential imposed by the agreed to price conditions on the sensitive services. It is interesting to note at least two important aspects of this approach:

1. It is in the carriers' best interest to assure that certain elements of competition exist in order to achieve the required critical mass of deregulated services necessary to provide the flexibility to recover the needed subsidies, since regulatory flexibility and deregulation is typically only permitted where adequate competition exists.

2. The approach allows for market segmentation by customer/customer class as well as service (i.e., does not prohibit discriminatory pricing).

The second element is essential for the carrier to compete on the basis of geography, customer size, and specific customer requirements and capabilities, and still be able to generate the necessary revenue to cover the regulatory cost elements not imposed on competitors.

It is also important to note that the approach gives few, if any, protections to business customers beyond the attempt to guarantee competitive choices. Business is generally on its own to procure telecommunications services as it would any other service necessary to the conduct of business — by negotiation and prudent procurement practices. The problem is that at the present time, many businesses and institutions may not be well prepared technically, administratively, or strategically to do this, and the costs for not doing it well can be great. These are particularly salient issues for many libraries and academic institutions, and constitute a major driving force behind the current interest in networks and networking among these organizations.

Bypass

To the extent that pricing principles diverge significantly from underlying costs in the absence of a highly regulated environment, opportunities can arise for a user, or in some instances another carrier, to provide alternative facilities to those provided by a given carrier at reduced cost. Use of alternative facilities is often called bypass, although the FCC has defined bypass in narrower terms.

> *Bypass is the transmission of long-distance messages that do not use the facilities of local telephone companies available to the general public, but that could use such facilities. [FCC, Bypass...,* 1984, p. 7].

As a specific consequence of Divestiture — the legal separation of the IXCs from the local telephone companies — and the failure to move to substantially cost-based pricing, a significant revenue shortfall for the support of the local telephone network resulted. This shortfall had previously been offset by cross-subsidization from long-distance services which were then within the sole purview of an integrated carrier (e.g., Bell System). To remedy the shortfall, the FCC ordered access charges paid to the local telephone company by the IXCs based on its use of the local network to originate and terminate long-distance traffic. In passing, it should be noted that these charges were designed to recover fixed, or so-called nontraffic sensitive (NTS) costs, but were actually assessed on the basis of minutes-of-use by the IXC as a mechanism of prorating the fees among the various interexchange network providers — a point of frequent confusion. Envisioned by the FCC to be a transitional measure that would fulfill the local telephone company revenue shortfall until the local network could be made more self-sufficient with the gradual increase of local rates — thus minimizing "rate shock" — these charges created problems of a different nature.

Not only is it possible for the IXCs to avoid payment of these fees by not using the facilities of the local telephone company, but since the usage is measured in the local telephone company switch, it is also possible to avoid certain of the fees by bypassing the switch — regardless of use of the local facilities.

Bypass has generally been divided into three categories:

1. Facilities bypass involves construction of alternative facilities by the user, or procurement of the facilities from other than the local telephone company, in order to gain access to the long-distance network of an IXC.

2. Service bypass is the procurement of such facilities from the local telephone company, but in such a manner as to connect directly to the IXC network, hence bypassing the local telephone company switch.

    In both facilities and service bypass, certain access fees are avoided, making the alternative financially attractive. Since the local telephone company facilities are generally not cost-based, it is often possible for larger users to construct or procure private facilities at a lesser rate than that charged by the local telephone company, giving an added financial incentive for facilities bypass.

3. End-to-end bypass, such as the use of direct point-to-point satellite links or private fiber-optic or microwave systems, simply bypasses both the local carrier and the long-distance carrier. This has the economic advantages of facilities bypass as well as any economies that the user can generate with regard to the IXC element.

    Bypass can also be classified as:

*   Economic

*   Uneconomic

Economic bypass is characterized, as described earlier, by economic incentives. There are, however, other reasons that a user might consider bypass. These may include the requirement for capacity or functionality that is not available from the public carrier, or may reflect an attempt on the part of the user to provide a degree of stability with regard to operating costs or operational flexibility not possible — or not likely — in a regulated environment. Whatever the reason, bypass for other than purely economic reasons is usually classified as uneconomic bypass.

Current Issues and Future Change

The issues and elements discussed above have given rise to the telecommunications environment and infrastructure as it exists today, and suggest the likelihood of certain changes important to the future telecommunications environment. Networks, including those used to support library and information system applications, will find it necessary to operate effectively within this environment — both currently and in the future. Some of the more important changes and probable impacts, as seen by the author, are presented and discussed below.

Special Access

Special access facilities are provided by the local telephone company to connect user communications equipment to long-distance facilities on a dedicated basis. Examples of special access facilities are private-line local channels used to connect long-distance private lines to local user equipment, or dedicated circuits used to connect user equipment directly to a long-distance carrier's network. These facilities can generally be distinguished by the fact that they are not directly connected to the local switched telephone network, although they sometimes carry traffic indirectly to the local switched telephone network through connections to PBXs (so-called leaky PBXs) or through use of the long-distance carrier's network (i.e., the issue of IXCs not blocking intraLATA traffic). Although the FCC has attempted to recover lost NTS revenue for such use of the local network through imposition of a special access surcharge currently set at $25 per end per month (i.e., some special access circuits have more than two ends, for example multidrop lines), this mechanism has not proved to be totally effective.

Certain private-line configurations are incapable of leaking traffic onto the local switched network, and the FCC has allowed exemption from the special access surcharge upon certification by the user that the circuit in question cannot leak. The exemption process, however, has been ineffective and has resulted in abuse, since in most instances it is not possible for the local telephone company to verify the claim of exemption without actually monitoring the use of the circuit, which is prohibited due to privacy considerations. It is likely that the FCC will eliminate, or substantially modify, the special access surcharge in the future — either directly, or indirectly through other regulatory proceedings. This could have a negative impact on private networks, since any resulting revenue shortfall would be recovered by some broader-based mechanism, potentially putting an additional cost burden on private networks which are currently exempt from the surcharge.

Special access rates have increased significantly over the past several years. As an example, OCLC users have experienced increases of more than 60% in the local access portion of their private-line facilities. Separation of intraLATA and interLATA services under terms of the Modified Final Judgment (MFJ) as a result of the breakup of the Bell system, and the necessary restructuring of tariffs contributed in a major way toward these increases. Prior to this restructuring, elements of local access had been substantially subsidized by interexchange service revenue. With the post-Divestiture restructuring, the FCC moved these elements closer to the recognized cost to provide these services. The need to recover more of these costs from the local subscribers and business has resulted in a disproportionate shift of this burden to special access services rather than to the local ratepayer. With the current movement toward deregulation and strategic pricing, small- to medium-sized organizations can continue to expect to bear a disproportionate share of this cost burden. In general, special access rates are expected to experience significant increases in the short- to intermediate-term future. This effect will likely be mitigated only to the extent that the local telephone companies are able to streamline their operations, resulting in underlying cost reductions, and hence an overall decrease in revenue requirements.

Switched Access

Costs associated with the provision of local telephone service are still subsidized by interexchange services. These subsidies are expected to be significantly reduced, and most probably eliminated over the next few years. The costs to support the local telephone network will subsequently need to be recovered at the local level. What is not clear at this time is exactly how these costs will be recovered. The author's best judgment is that a proportionate share of these costs will eventually be recovered from the local subscriber (i.e., residential and single-line business subscriber) base, but that this shift will be more gradual than the shift of the costs to the local level. This implies that certain local services (e.g., special access) may be forced to bear a disproportionate share of these costs early on. It appears quite clear however, switched access costs will increase over the next three to five years or so.

In addition to the loss of subsidies for local services, significant changes in allowed depreciation practices will result in increased nontraffic-sensitive (NTS) cost elements, not only as the depreciation cost surplus is eliminated, but also as more appropriate depreciation procedures are applied to the acquisition of substantial telephone plant and equipment which will be needed to modernize many local networks. This has resulted in growth of the NTS cost elements in the recent past, and is expected to continue to put upward pressure on switched access rates. Again, the only apparent means by which these increases might be mitigated is through possible reductions in the underlying cost structures of the local carriers through streamlining their operations.

It should also be noted that when the FCC ordered long-distance carriers to pay access charges for connecting to the local switched telephone network, the Commission provided an exemption for enhanced service providers, including the so-called value added networks (VANs). The reason given by the FCC for the exemption, which it considered temporary, was the fear that such a sudden and significant increase in the cost structure (i.e., rate shock) for these VANs could cause potentially irreparable damage to emerging information services. Nearly four years later, on June 10, 1987, the FCC proposed to remove this exemption, arguing that the VANs had had ample time to restructure their businesses and that the local ratepayer was in effect subsidizing the VANs' use of the local network, something the Commission could no longer condone. Elimination of this exemption would have had a significant effect on the cost structure of the VANs and subsequently on the prices they charge their users — many of whom are libraries. After a groundswell of opposition to the elimination of this waiver from users, ESPs, Congress, and others, the FCC subsequently withdrew the proposal. The waiver could subsequently be eliminated in the future by the FCC, but a more likely course would be to increase revenues via other means — possibly with the new open network architecture (ONA) tariffs that are being formulated as the manuscript for this book is being completed.

Local Measured Service

As state regulators put pressure on local telephone companies to restrain the rate-of-rise of local-service rates, most likely in return for pricing flexibility or deregulation in other areas, this restraint is expected to take the form of usage-sensitive service charges in many jurisdictions. By imposing mandatory local measured service (LMS), the carrier will argue that the local subscriber can control his or her telephone service expenditures and significantly reduce costs. In fact, taken on face value, this is probably the case. There are however, several inherent problems with mandatory LMS, as compared with flat-rate unmeasured local service (i.e., unlimited local calls) that is currently the more general practic— or at least a subscriber option — in most jurisdictions.

It is straightforward to gauge the impact of rate changes for flat-rate service. With LMS, however, there is significant opportunity for the carrier to manipulate numerous parameters that can impact the overall costs to a particular subscriber in ways that can be complex and difficult to predict. Among the parameters that may be used to determine LMS costs are number, distance, and duration of calls, as well as time of day. Also, business customers tend to place more calls, and where dial-access to computers is involved, the calls tend to be substantially longer in duration; hence business tends to bear more of the burden for the support of the local telephone network under LMS schemes, even though the NTS costs are by definition not usage sensitive. This can result in business subscribers bearing a substantially disproportionate share of the cost to provide, for example, local-loop facilities — even though the actual cost of these facilities is the same, whether they are used to capacity or not used at all. The impact of mandatory LMS on libraries that use the switched network to access information services, etc., can be potentially devastating. There is some experience, however, that hints that a major segment of the local-subscriber base may be opposed to mandatory LMS, and any vocal opposition may forestall mandatory LMS in these jurisdictions — at least in the near term.

Local Area Data Transport

Many jurisdictions currently have in place, or are planning to implement local packet networks, often called local area data transport (LADT) systems (mentioned earlier in this book). A major element of subscriber access cost is related to "subscriber plant" (e.g., the telephone wires connecting the subscriber to the telephone office). In the majority of cases, this facility is in place and typically used less than 5% to 10% of the time, and to only a small fraction of its potential capacity. Most of these facilities are capable of carrying information at many times the rate typically used for voice conversations. Through use of modern technology (e.g., data-over-voice, or DOV, multiplexors), and with a relatively moderate investment, these facilities can be made to provide simultaneous access to a local packet network. This approach is expected to serve as the foundation for the evolution of various local telephone company-provided LADT services, and will enable the provision of high-speed data access at marginal cost using mostly in-place facilities. LADT is also considered to be an early forerunner of the evolving integrated services digital network (ISDN). LADT networks are expected to provide an economic access alternative to long-distance private and public data networks in some locations in the near term, with increasing availability and more competitive prices in the intermediate term. For example, a VAN or information service may simply connect its network to the LADT network, thus allowing convenient access by LADT subscribers. Long term, LADT is expected to become less attractive as ISDN evolves as a viable alternative.

Long-Haul Capacity

Long-haul capacity will substantially increase over the next few years with construction and operation of significant amounts of new capacity — much of which will be fiber optic. The outlook for satellite facilities is currently less optimistic. As traffic is shifted to fiber networks from satellites, and as new traffic — particularly on high-density routes — is initiated on fiber networks, investors can be expected to become more apprehensive toward satellite technology. Digital terrestrial fiber facilities are expected to become increasingly dominant through the remainder of this century. Nonetheless, satellite transmission will play an important role with regard to certain aspects of the long-haul market, particularly in more remote areas where fiber has not penetrated, and may not penetrate for some time to come. Very small aperture terminal (VSAT) satellite earthstations can be expected to provide an attractive alternative in these regions where data rates are not excessive.

Competition is expected to force long-haul capacity to the status of a commodity — particularly on high-density routes — where moderate-to-large units of capacity can be accommodated (e.g., 45 Mbps T-3 and above, and possibly as small as 1.544 Mbps T-1). Even in smaller capacity units, competition along these routes is expected to force prices closer to marginal costs and result in reductions over current long-haul prices. Market segmentation may keep long-haul prices artificially high in some geographic areas for the near future, but in the longer run, downward trends should come to bear on these routes as well. This will offer significant opportunities for organizations (e.g., libraries and institutions) to band together and consolidate their respective telecommunications traffic on common networks in order to take advantage of these high-capacity facilities.

Therefore, reductions are expected in long-haul facilities prices, although the extent of these reductions is expected to vary by market segment. Increasingly, as long-haul capacity becomes more of a commodity, more unbundling of capacity from other services offered by the carrier is expected. Pricing for each of these elements is expected to move toward marginal cost levels, at a rate and to the extent competitive forces dictate. This will put the onus on the user to procure these services effectively.

Deregulation

The author expects to see significant, and in some cases total deregulation of telecommunications products and services in most jurisdictions over the course of the next five years or so. In fact, the Department of Commerce, the Department of Justice, and even MCI has recommended movement toward deregulation of AT&T. Several states have already proposed or enacted telecommunications deregulation legislation. Telecommunications markets are also expected to be segmented on the basis of product or service, market area, customer or class of customer, and geography — particularly with regard to dominant competitive forces within a given area. As a result, prices for a given service may vary significantly between localities and customers. With the advent of strategic pricing, carriers will initially attempt to recover subsidies for local subscriber service from other products and services when and where competition, or lack thereof, allows. The historical market segmentation by product or service alone is not expected to suffice in the new environment, and multiple levels of market segmentation are expected to result. This is expected to be particularly important for evolving networks as they formulate their telecommunications-related product and service cost/price strategies.

Procurement

As deregulation proceeds, carriers will increasingly be freed from tariff constraints. With the advent of further deregulation over the next few years, telecommunications and related product and service prices, terms, and conditions are expected to increasingly be negotiated on a case-by-case basis — particularly where the magnitude of potential revenue is large. This will place the onus on the customer to formulate effective procurement strategies and tactics, package procurements effectively, and negotiate optimum results. In addition, the administrative aspects of procurement, operation, maintenance, etc., of these elements will increase significantly. This will be particularly evident as carriers unbundle support and other administrative services. Simply tracking which elements are related to which supplier, the disparate procedures of various suppliers and their respective contracts, etc., can be expected to take on significantly greater scope.

As telecommunications equipment and services continue to be deregulated, organizations may no longer be protected by the applicable state and federal tariffs to the extent to which they have been in the past with regard to procuring telecommunications and related equipment and services. Prior to deregulation and competition, there was little or no choice regarding service and equipment rates and terms; the current tariffs, scrutinized by the various regulatory agencies, provided the equivalent of a legal contract between purchaser and supplier. Organizations need to be vigilant to ensure that their procurement capabilities and procedures appropriately reflect the changing telecommunications regulatory and market environments, particularly as contractual and legal protections might be a concern.

Modified Final Judgment

The Modified Final Judgment (MFJ) specifically prohibits the Bell operating companies from engaging in interexchange telecommunications, information services and the manufacture of equipment. These are often referred to as the MFJ core restrictions. The MFJ contains an escape clause, however, that permits the BOCs to obtain waivers of the restrictions from the court. With mounting consensus in Congress, the FCC, the White House, the Department of Justice, the Department of Commerce, and of course AT&T, the Bell operating companies, and even MCI, that relaxation or elimination of some, or all of the core constraints is needed, the question appears to be "when and how much" rather than "whether" the MFJ should be reconsidered. A significant presence by AT&T or the Bell operating companies in the provision of information could have a major impact on organizations providing information services, or aspiring to provide these services, including libraries.

Integrated Services Digital Network

Increasingly, users of telecommunications services need to transmit information in a variety of forms: voice, data, image, video, etc. More often than not, dedicated physical facilities are currently required for each type of communications. The management of multiple application-dependent networks is operationally complex and the redundancies are costly.

Digital switching, digital transmission, and a modern signaling and control subnetwork are the building blocks for what is known as the integrated services digital network (ISDN). ISDN promises the following benefits for telecommunications users:

1. No need for separate networks

2.   No need for modems

3.   The ability to simultaneously send different types of messages over the same line

4.   Faster, clearer, more error-free transmission

5.   Customer control of services available on particular lines

Two prerequisites of the ISDN are pervasive implementation of digital transmission and digital switching technologies. This implementation is currently occurring at a rapid pace, and the ISDN is expected to be widely available beginning in about 1990, although limited availability in some places is expected sooner.

A ubiquitous, universally and economically available, national public voice network has in the past served to relegate private voice networks to a limited domain. Private voice networks have generally been found to be effective where large traffic volumes are involved or special needs (e.g., security) are important. The attractiveness of even these networks is being reduced with the evolution of so-called virtual private networks such as the AT&T Software Defined Network (SDN) offering. Using the inherent intelligence of the network switch, the carrier can provide many of the advantages of a private-line network using the national long-distance network. The user appears to have a dedicated private network, while in fact the traffic is actually carried on the public network. This enables the carrier to take advantage of the economies of scope and scale of this network.

On the other hand, the lack of such a national data network has spawned a variety of different private data networks. With the transition from a basically analog switching and transmission infrastructure to an all digital network, ISDN proffers the evolution of a ubiquitous and widely available integrated public network. The economies of scope and scale ultimately available in such a network would seem to call into question the long-term outlook for many private data networks. Private networks that survive in an ISDN era will very likely have special requirements not readily met by the ISDN network.

Impacts

Many changes have already taken place within the telecommunications infrastructure, and still more change is foreseen in the coming months and years. This change has already had significant impact on library and information systems, and additional impact is nearly assured. It may be beneficial to focus on specific impacts expected to be felt by:

1.   National online information servers, such as BRS, CompuServe, Dialog, Mead Data Central, OCLC, or RLG

2.   Local online information providers, including libraries that are, or are planning to be, online

3.   Local and interexchange telecommunications carriers, such as AT&T and the Bell operating companies, that may vigorously pursue the business of providing information

4.   Users of information

National Online Information Servers

Most national online information servers deliver their services using either a private data network, value-added network (VAN), or both. The impact of change in the telecommunications arena on these organizations will be both short term and long term. In the short term, the major impacts will be a substantial increase in the cost of delivering their services and the potential for significant increases in the cost of overhead associated with procurement and operation of their delivery systems.

The increase in the cost of access to VANs and the potentially devastating effects of mandatory LMS on the cost of access to the VANs for computerized applications cannot be overlooked, or underestimated. Significant cost increases for private-line access will come from:

1. The shifting of burden for the support of the local network to special access services

2. Deregulation

3. Strategic pricing

Although long-distance private-line facilities are expected to decrease in cost along high-traffic-density routes when procured in large volume, most of the national providers are neither positioned to be able to use these facilities effectively, nor do they possess the consolidated traffic volumes to take significant advantage of these savings. In addition, rate deaveraging and strategic pricing can result in significant cost increases for certain customers, or in certain locations. This could present the potential for loss of business on a scale that might not be expected when only average telecommunications cost increases are considered, and points out the importance of careful consideration of telecommunications pricing strategies by these organizations (e.g., implementation of average or national pricing strategies). Increased overhead costs can also be expected to contribute to increased service prices. Therefore, the short- to intermediate-term outlook for the impacts on these organizations has a negative potential — particularly when considered in light of the emergence of alternative information delivery mechanisms such as local CD-ROM database systems, etc.

In the longer term, the emergence of a ubiquitous ISDN network could present a more positive outlook for these organizations. It will be to the advantage of these organizations, however, to consider the potential of the ISDN network, which is evolving in compliance with the International Standards Organization (ISO) Open Systems Interconnection (OSI) model, as a primary delivery mechanism in their evolving system strategies, in order to take maximum advantage of this future opportunity.

It should also be pointed out that the accommodation and use of shared regional, national, and international telecommunications networks by these organizations could help to bridge the gap between short term and long term. This mechanism offers the opportunity to consolidate both traffic, and support and administrative overhead.

Local Online Information Providers

Local online information providers face many of the same issues as the national systems, to the extent that they utilize the local exchange network for delivery of their services. In particular, the shift of the burden of support for the local network to the local level will result in increased delivery costs. This may be particularly true for local systems, since they generally cannot generate the economies of scale of the larger national systems over which to amortize a proportionately larger fixed administrative and support overhead cost. Mandatory LMS, to the extent it exists in the local jurisdiction, will also contribute to increased cost to deliver online information using the local network.

Improvements in both capability and cost of private institutional networks (i.e., wired campus, etc.), brought about primarily by advances in technology, may offer significant potential opportunities for some local online providers. It may be possible for these organizations to take advantage of significant investments made by a parent institution in modern telecommunications technology to deliver information-based online services at marginal cost.

In the intermediate to long term, developments in the areas of LADT and ISDN can be expected to offer the same advantages to local providers as to national providers, at least for local access. As with the national systems, this also suggests consideration of these delivery mechanisms in the planning and design of evolving local online information systems.

Local and Interexchange Telecommunications Carriers

A concern on the part of the court that AT&T and the Bell operating companies (BOCs) could use their significant economies of scale and their control of the telecommunications network to inhibit competition in the area of provision of information — as well as a recognition that the modern switching equipment being implemented at ratepayer expense could be used to facilitate these activities — has led to the prohibition against providing these services contained in the MFJ. Both AT&T and the BOCs would appear to have moved judiciously to position themselves for vigorous entry into this area. It is likely that the MFJ constraint will be lifted, in part or in whole, within the foreseeable future, and these companies will move aggressively into the area of information provision. Initial competitive thrusts are likely to be in lucrative commercial markets. There is little doubt, however, that if they are successful they will move toward lower-margin markets as they seek to expand market share. One thing is for certain, current and aspiring information service providers will be well advised to carefully consider the competitive implications of entry into the information services market place by these organizations, since many, if not most of the future developments within the telecommunications infrastructure foreseen by the author are favorable, or at least not as unfavorable, to these organizations.

Users of Information

Much has been written about the impacts of change on users of information. Advances within the telecommunications infrastructure will move toward enabling the user to gain access to ever-increasing amounts of information in expanding forms and formats. In the nearer term, the likely developments discussed above will contribute to increases in cost for delivery of that information. On the other hand, increases in functionality of terminal and workstation equipment at ever-decreasing cost may help to offset these cost increases to some extent. Also, investment by major institutions in local telecommunications network technology can be expected to further access to information by their users at marginal cost.

In the longer term, evolution of the ISDN network could further empower the user to gain access to a wider body of information at more reasonable cost. Although not within the scope of this book, this raises strategic questions for information intermediaries and information providers alike.

Summary

Much like a whirlwind sight-seeing tour, the author has attempted to present a comprehensive — if somewhat superficial — overview of the telecommunications infrastructure, the forces at work remolding it, and some of the likely outcomes and impacts of this process. In summary, several points might be made. The telecommunications infrastructure is undergoing revolutionary change and development which will have far-reaching impacts. This might be likened to the kind of change wrought by the evolution of the transportation infrastructure with the development of a nationwide interstate highway system, or intercontinental air service. Existing delivery systems, such as the railroads and steamships, were negatively impacted, while truck, automobile and airplane design and production, fuel distribution systems, and even population densities were impacted in ways that were often unanticipated.

The next three to five years or so are expected to bring turbulent times to information-system-related enterprise that depends upon the existing telecommunications infrastructure for access to and delivery of information. Access and delivery costs are expected to increase, and to the extent that these costs form the basis for related service costs, these costs will increase as well. The impact will be proportional to the ratio of delivery to total service costs. Interestingly, this will likely put low service-cost organizations at a comparative disadvantage.

As the transition period passes and the environment becomes more stable, the overall outlook would seem to be more favorable; however, as was the case with the railroads and trucking industry, the relative positioning, and indeed the existence, of some services may be expected to change. Without a doubt, the present environment constitutes the most exciting and dynamic period in the history of telecommunications.

"We shall not cease from exploration, and the end of all
our exploring will be to arrive where we started,
and to know the place for the first time."
(Little Gidding) T.S. Eliot [1888–1965]

Recent Developments Within the Public Network

Recent developments within the public network have brought about changes with potentially significant implications for certain users, including library and information systems professionals. This chapter is intended to briefly review some of these more recent developments.

Operator Services

It is estimated that between 12 and 13 million operator-assisted telephone calls are placed in the United States every day. With a few exceptions, prior to Divestiture — the breakup of the Bell System discussed elsewhere in this book — the user simply dialed *0* and was connected with an AT&T operator. The world of operator services has now become considerably more complicated, and unfortunately, this trend will likely continue. At latest count, there were upwards of 60 companies providing operator services. Too often, users may not be aware that more than one operator service is available, let alone know which one they want to use, or how to reach this service — if indeed they can reach their preferred service at all.

Often, significant differences exist in:

1. The quality of the operator service

2. The quality of the carried call

3. The cost of the carried call, including the surcharge for the operator assistance, that can be as much as 200% or more greater than the rates charged by AT&T

4. The functionality of the service, including the capability to complete and bill a call

Universities, among other organizations, as well as proprietors of locations where pay telephones might be located, have become targets for the newer operator-services providers, and even if a library has not yet been affected, it may be impacted in the future. Further, anyone who travels, as many library and information science professionals do, is well advised to understand what is happening in this area.

The Impact of Divestiture

At Divestiture, AT&T was assigned Bell System operator-services facilities and associated personnel. Many other companies now provide these services, including: other long-distance companies, independent telephone companies, so-called resellers of long-distance service, and so-called alternative operator services (AOSs). In addition, the Bell operating companies (BOCs) were permitted by the Divestiture agreement to provide operator services for intraLATA calls (i.e., calls within a local access and transport area, or LATA), and are now beginning to provide these services. Where the local telephone company provides these intraLATA operator services, dialing *0* usually connects the user with the local operator service, and it may be necessary to dial *00* to reach the long-distance carrier of the user's choice.

Switched Network Architecture

Before going any further, a brief digression into the architecture of the switched network is in order if one is to sort out the various aspects of operator services. The local exchange carriers (LECs), which include the 22 BOCs and the 1,400 or so independent local telephone companies, provide access for interexchange, or long-distance, carriers (IXCs) to the LECs' subscribers within each LATA. It is usually possible to connect to the local switches in one of two ways:

• A line-side connection

• A trunk-side connection

Line-side connections are typically used to connect the subscribers' telephone instruments to the LEC's switch, while trunk-side connections are usually, but not always used to connect the LEC's switch to other switches or the interLATA network. There are two basic differences between these two methods of connection. The line-side connections are provided over a single two-wire loop, while trunk-side connections consist of so-called four-wire circuits, isolating inbound from outbound signals. Thus, the trunk-side connection provides a nominally higher quality connection. The second difference results from the way in which signaling information is communicated, as well as the inherent capability of the LEC's switch to provide certain functions on trunk-side connections that are not available on the line side of the switch.

Feature Group Access

After Divestiture and the advent of equal access, which was designed to ensure that all IXCs received equal treatment regarding access to the LECs' subscribers, four classes of access to the LECs' switches were defined; the so-called Feature Groups (FGs) A through D. FGA is a line-side connection. To gain access to the network of an IXC that has chosen FGA, the subscriber must typically dial a seven-digit access number, receive a second dial tone (from the IXC's switch), dial an authorization code (usually five digits) for billing purposes, and then dial the full number of the party being called (i.e., seven-digit IXC access number + five-digit billing authorization code + area code + seven-digit called number). Since the LEC's switch usually cannot pass pulse-dialed codes from a line-side (local caller) to line-side (FGA IXC) connection, the caller is often required to have dual-tone multifrequency (DTMF), or so-called Touch-Tone dialing capability, at least after receiving the IXC's dial tone.

FGB access provides a trunk-side, rather than line-side connection to the IXC's network. In this case, to gain access the subscriber dials a seven-digit number of the form *950-10XX,* where the *XX* is a two-digit number identifying the IXC (not to be confused with the five-digit *10XXX* IXC codes discussed later). Depending upon whether the capability is available on the particular LEC's switch or has been purchased by the IXC, pulse dialing and automatic identification of the calling subscriber to the IXC's switch may be provided by the LEC's switch, in which case the caller might be able to use a pulse-dialing instrument, or might not be required to dial the additional authorization code. FGC is the trunk-side access provided to AT&T prior to Divestiture and is available to AT&T only, on an interim basis, until FGD can be made available.

FGD is a new trunk-side interconnection arrangement designed to meet the equal access requirements of the Divestiture agreement. When IXCs use FGD, subscribers can presubscribe to the services of a specific IXC of their choice (often called Dial-One or 1-plus dialing), whereafter the LEC routes long-distance traffic to this IXC when the subscriber dials *1* plus the long-distance number. If a subscriber wishes a different IXC to carry a specific call — regardless of any presubscription choice the subscriber may have made — the subscriber can dial a five-digit IXC access code of the form *10XXX,* where the *XXX* designates a specific IXC, followed by the long-distance number (e.g., 10XXX + 1 + area code + seven-digit number), and the LEC will route this traffic to the IXC specified by the access code. This capability, which is neither widely publicized nor understood, is sometimes referred to as Gypsy Calling, and enables the subscriber to chose which IXC will carry each and every call on the basis of best price and service according to the specific circumstances. It should be noted that not all IXCs have subscribed to FGD access in all LATAs, and FGD is not yet universally available, so it may not be possible to reach a given IXC by dialing their 10XXX code from all geographic locations.

Accessing Different Long-Distance Services

Presubscription is merely a subscriber convenience, relieving the subscriber from having to dial a five-digit IXC access code for the majority of long-distance calls, and not a commitment to a particular carrier for all of the subscriber's long-distance traffic — regardless of what the presubscribed carrier might wish to have the subscriber believe. Billing for both presubscribed and Gypsy calls is usually handled in a similar manner by the local telephone company, but some long-distance carriers have chosen to bill the customer directly. It is also usually unnecessary to have a previous arrangement with the IXC to place these calls, particularly with the major carriers, but sometimes the IXC will provide certain discounts or reduced rates when such an advanced arrangement is in effect.

Putting aside for the moment the further complications involving certain hospitals, universities, hotels, pay phones, etc., where AOSs are involved, there are at least three ways of accessing operator services. Assuming the availability of equal access — which now includes nearly all major metropolitan areas and many rural areas — the operator service provided by any FGD IXC (not all IXCs provide operator services) can be accessed by dialing the five-digit IXC access code plus *0* (i.e., 10XXX + 0). Provided the LEC does not provide its own intraLATA operator services, the subscriber can usually reach the operator service of a presubscribed IXC by simply dialing *0*. Where the LEC provides intraLATA operator service, the LEC service is most often reached by dialing *0*, while it is usually necessary to dial *00* to reach the operator service of the presubscribed IXC. As noted, this assumes that the IXC provides long-distance operator services, which not all do.

Operator-Assisted Calls

Operator-assisted calls generally fall into two classes: the so-called 0-minus type, where the caller dials the operator and waits for the operator to come onto the line; and 0-plus calls, which involve dialing *0* plus a destination number, and then giving a credit-card number to the operator (or with some equipment, dialing the credit-card number when a so-called *bong tone* is received). Typically, a caller who is traveling places 0-plus calls. Such calls are handled by the operator service of the IXC to which the calling line is presubscribed, and not by the operator service of the IXC to which the call will be billed. Except under certain circumstances — generally where AOSs are involved — it may be possible to circumvent this problem by dialing the five-digit IXC access code prior to dialing *0* (i.e., 10XXX + 0 + area code + seven-digit number).

To circumvent the 0-plus problem, in August of 1987 Ameritech asked the Federal Communications Commission (FCC) to authorize the LECs to develop interconnected operator call handling networks. Under the plan, operator calls dialed without IXC access codes would be routed to a BOC line information database (LIDB), that would identify the preferred IXC of the party to whom the call would be billed, and the call would then be routed to that IXC. This proposal has been vigorously opposed by the major IXCs, among others, on the grounds that it would violate the prohibition against BOC interLATA long-distance services contained in the Divestiture agreement. Meanwhile in October of 1987, AT&T asked the FCC for permission to provide a new Hospitality Network Service (HNS) that would offer high-volume long-distance traffic aggregators, such as hotels/motels, hospitals and universities, reduced rates on direct-dialed 1-plus traffic (i.e., AT&T pre-subscribed traffic) and commissions on 0-plus calls in exchange for a commitment to channel specific volumes of traffic to AT&T. This proposal was subsequently approved by the FCC in July of 1988.

Long-Distance Commissions

Prior to 1981, AT&T had paid commissions to hotels, hospitals, and other similar organizations. This was justified by AT&T on the grounds that the FCC prohibited resale of telecommunications services, and that the added overhead of collecting fees for telephone calls meant that many of these organizations would not otherwise have provided telephones for their clients. When, in 1981, the FCC decided to allow the resale of switched telephone services, AT&T announced it would no longer pay these commissions. In the absence of the AT&T commissions, private operator-services companies were able to convince hospitals, hotels/motels, universities, and similar organizations to let them perform these services. These AOS firms could purchase bulk long-distance facilities from AT&T and/or other IXCs (e.g., usually WATS and/or private lines) at discounted rates, provide commissions to their client organizations, and still turn a profit. An FCC decision in 1984 cleared the way for interstate competition in the pay telephone industry, that proved to be an enticing and profitable business into which the AOS firms also expanded. AOS providers have captured about 4.9% of the operator-assisted call market since 1985, and this is forecast to grow to nearly 12% by 1993.

AOS Problems

The typical AOS operation captures long-distance and operator-assisted calls at the hotel/motel, hospital, or university, or at the pay telephone. This traffic is often "back-hauled," or carried back to the AOS's operation center, which may be located thousands of miles from the source of the calls. This may also be done via FGA using auto-dialing equipment, with subsequent potential degradation of both call response time and transmission quality. With or without operator intervention, the calls are then placed on the long-distance facilities owned, leased, and/or chosen by the AOS. There are numerous opportunities for problems with this approach, which can be grouped into three general categories:

1. Charges and billing

2. Capabilities offered

3. Quality of the services rendered

Back-Hauled Calls

Since AOS services are generally not regulated, the caller is at the mercy of the providers. This can be particularly problematic since the owner of the hotel, pay telephone location, etc., the AOS company, and the IXC are generally all involved with a "piece of the action." Further, the customer often is unaware of what has happened until it comes time to check out of the hotel, or worse yet, until the telephone credit-card bill arrives. To further complicate matters, the bill itself may not only be unduly expensive, but confusing as well. As an example, a credit-card call placed from a hotel phone in Chicago to a Milwaukee destination may be back-hauled by the AOS to Tulsa, Oklahoma, using their facilities, handed off to the IXC in Tulsa, and completed in Milwaukee. The credit-card bill would then likely contain an operator-assisted call surcharge that would cover the overhead of back-hauling the call to Tulsa and a long-distance charge from Tulsa to Milwaukee. The traveler might argue, "But I've never been to Tulsa!" *Surprise!*

Splashed Calls

A similar situation can result when a caller, realizing that a call is not being handled by the IXC of their choice, requests that the call be transferred to a specific IXC. These so-called splashed calls are usually transferred to the requested IXC at the location nearest the AOS's switch, which may be thousands of miles from the location of the origination of the call, hence resulting in an apparent call from the location of the AOS's switch to the destination point of the call. Again, the Chicago to Milwaukee call may appear on the bill as originating in Tulsa!

Circumventing the Local Network

In many instances involving AOSs, the long-distance traffic never sees the local telephone company switch, but rather is piped directly into the AOS's switch. Hence, attempting to escape the problem by dialing an IXC access code can be fruitless. It may be possible to get a local outside line from a hotel phone, and then dial the access code, but since most hotel/AOS switches examine the dialed number and trap nonlocal traffic, there are no guarantees. Since some long-distance carriers provide toll-free 800 or 950 numbers, it may be possible to bypass the AOS by using one of these numbers if you subscribe to the services of one of these carriers, but again, there are no guarantees since the call may be trapped. With pay phones, this can be even more problematic.

Uncompleted Calls

Probably most aggravating are situations wherein the underlying IXC chosen by the AOS does not have total geographic coverage. This can result in a real "catch-22" situation; there can be absolutely no way to get from here to there. The AOS captures the long-distance call, and subsequently can't complete it. Further, users can't get access to their IXCs of choice because the AOS intercepts the attempt. Also, for a variety of reasons, the AOS may not accept telephone credit cards, or possibly even bank credit cards, and since users may not be able to get to their chosen IXCs, they're out of luck! In addition, it is possible to handle 0-plus calls completely by computer. In some instances, equipment is used that captures 0-plus calls, but when a user wants to place a 0-minus call, they are passed off to yet another operator service. Among other things, this generally does little to contribute to transmission quality or call response time.

Determining When a Call Is Completed

In many instances the AOS does not have the capability to determine when a call has or has not been completed, and typically assumes that calls greater than a certain duration (often in the neighborhood of 40 seconds) were completed. In these instances, it is possible to be billed for an uncompleted call if more than the allotted time is allowed to elapse between the time the call was initiated and the time the unanswered call was terminated. This can also result in a completed call not being billed if its entire duration is less than the allotted time.

Problems in an Emergency

The problems that I have described are generally aggravations, inconveniences, and/or additional expenses for the user. There is another potential problem, particularly where public pay telephones such as those that may be located in libraries are involved, that can be a serious threat. Since pay telephones are often a vital link in serious emergency situations, an operator 3,000 miles away accepting calls from all across the nation, most likely totally unfamiliar with the local environment and possibly undertrained, may not be too helpful. Further, as discussed previously, it may not be possible to reach the local telephone company directly from the pay telephone in a timely manner, if at all.

Service Quality

Quality of service can also be a problem. The added routing hops that can result when the AOS is located at a distant location, as well as the insertion of the additional equipment into the loop, can result in degradation of transmission quality. In addition, inadequate equipment, use of FGA access, understaffing, or lack of adequate training, may be more likely with smaller companies operating on tight margins. As mentioned, any shortcomings of the underlying IXC may also come into play. With the exception of a few state commissions that regulate the access to pay phones and intrastate competition, the operator-services industry is controlled only by itself and the marketplace.

Calling Number Identification

A widely available feature in the public telephone network, but one not so widely understood by the general public, is calling party number identification, also known as automatic number identification or ANI (pronounced "Annie"). This feature can be used to provide the identity of the calling party to the called party, at least in terms of the telephone number, directly from the telephone network before the call is answered. An example is one of the new Bell Atlantic CLASS (Custom Local Area Signal Services) services being offered in New Jersey that displays the local calling number on the called party's telephone. A similar caller identification service has also been offered by Southern Bell in Florida. Since this information can be put to any number of uses, this capability is raising questions regarding the rights of a calling party to remain anonymous.

Anonymity

Anonymity is critical to the success of certain information "hot lines," such as drug-assistance hot lines, AIDS information hot lines, suicide prevention hot lines, and anonymous crime-solver hot lines, to name only a few. Telephone reference services provided by libraries also carry an element of anonymity for the patron. Currently, many callers to these services have an almost naive presumption of anonymity. As the discussion and debate surrounding ANI intensifies, it will become important to reassure callers of the commitment of these services to preserve the anonymity of the caller.

The anonymity of a calling party has, from the earliest days of telephony, been a matter of degrees. In the early days, a human operator could readily identify the calling party line from the physical location of the line termination on the operator's switchboard. It is also obvious that calling line identification has been used for toll-call billing purposes by the telephone company for many years. In the past, however, the telephone companies have carefully guarded the anonymity of the calling party, and this information has generally been used only for necessary billing functions and has not been made available to other parties. In fact, anyone who has experienced the need to trace a call can attest to the lack of facilities at the disposal of the telephone company to make this information available. This situation is, however, rapidly changing.

Station Message Detail Recording

Many businesses, institutions and other organizations use so-called station message detail recording, or SMDR, to keep track of calls placed from their telephone instruments. In fact it is more common than not for organizations using PBXs or telephone company-provided Centrex service to make use of these capabilities. These systems typically record such noncall-content information as the calling station, the number called, the date, time and duration of the call, and often PBX port and trunk utilization information, and are useful for management of the telephone facilities (e.g., capacity management, departmental budgetary "bill back," carrier-bill rectification, etc.) as well as allowing management to monitor employee calling. This information, however, seldom goes beyond the calling organization.

Evolution of ANI

Within a monolithic public monopoly telephone system, there was little need for the calling-party number to be forwarded with the calling information. With the advent of competition and the entry of other (than AT&T) long-distance carriers into the market place, it became necessary for these new carriers to gain access to the calling-party identity for their own billing purposes. Initially, this was accomplished through the use of user personal identification numbers, or PINs. Before a user could complete a call using one of these carriers, it was necessary for the user to dial his PIN, from which the carrier linked the call to the appropriate customer account for billing purposes. This process is, unfortunately, vulnerable to calling fraud and abuse. The requirement that non-AT&T customers dial extra digits, among other things, also gave AT&T a clear competitive advantage, which led to a mandate in the Bell System Divestiture agreement for equal access by all long-distance carriers to the local network. With the advent of equal access, long-distance, or inter-exchange carriers (IXCs) began to receive ANI information provided over Feature Group D (FGD) access to the local exchange carrier's (LEC's) local switch (Feature Groups A–D are the various options available for connecting to the local switch provided by equal access).

Although ANI has been available via this mechanism for some time, the information has generally been used by the IXC only on the "front end" of the calling process for billing purposes and then discarded. This remains the case today for the majority of toll-type services. Recently, however, MCI and AT&T have begun to collect ANI information on calls placed to certain 800 service numbers. This information is then turned over to the 800 subscriber in bulk form on a monthly basis, or in the case of a new AT&T integrated services digital network (ISDN) service, essentially in real time. These 800 services are frequently used by telemarketing operations.

Uses of ANI

An important example of the use of ANI information is the so-called enhanced 911 service, an emergency service that provides information, directly from the network, regarding the identity and location of a calling party to emergency service operators in many cities. A more questionable use might be the Bell Atlantic CLASS service described previously that identifies the calling party in a display window attached to the called party's telephone when the call is received, enabling the called party to answer or not answer the call — or possibly to ascertain that a spouse is not calling late from the office as claimed. ANI information might be used to trace computer hackers or obscene or abusive callers. It could be used by airlines, hotels, or other similar organizations, to provide faster and more efficient service by automatically displaying reservation and/or account information on an agent's computer terminal. This information could also be beneficial to credit-card verification services, since the identity of the calling merchant could be obtained directly from the network, speeding the verification process.

Local delivery services, such as pizza parlors, that are frequently troubled by prank orders, hope to use ANI to screen out these calls. National chains could also use the ANI information, provided to a central location via a national 800 service number, to dispatch the order to the nearest outlet location — customers frequently do not dial the closest franchise — and to use their computers to optimize delivery routes and scheduling, deriving a substantial competitive advantage while better serving their customers. The use of ANI information by telemarketing operations is limited only by their imagination and ingenuity — including processing and resale of the numbers.

ANI in Computer Networks

Another interesting concept involves the use of ANI information by major computer networks. It is possible for such a network to gain access to some or all local telephone network switches via Feature Group D. Terminal users that currently use dial access to reach the service, either directly or by use of a value-added network (VAN) such as Telenet, Tymnet, or CompuServe, could then presubscribe (i.e., Dial-One service) the local telephone line used by their terminals to the computer network (i.e., the computer network would become, in essence, the long-distance carrier of choice for that telephone line). Hence, when users (or more likely, their PC-based terminals) dialed *1,* they would be directly connected to the computer network. Dialing additional digits, which would be simply passed to the computer network along with the ANI information by the local telephone company switch, might be used to provide additional password identification, information regarding the particular service the user desired to access, etc. The ANI information provided to the computer network by the local telephone company's switch would uniquely identify the calling terminal, and greatly simplify the user logon process and subsequent billing. The potential for other uses, both benign and malevolent, is nearly boundless.

Telemarketing

Few telephone subscribers have escaped the purveyors of unsolicited sales telephone calls. These "junk" telephone calls can not only be a nuisance, coming at the most inconvenient times with uncanny regularity, but can also present serious problems under certain circumstances. Since libraries use telephone services extensively, these calls can range from minor annoyances, through significant consumers of staff time and resources, to serious problems with automated systems and delivery of automated services.

Technological advances have permitted telemarketing operations to become ever more sophisticated. Decreasing costs for this technology, as well as decreasing long-distance telephone rates, have enabled individual enterprises to extend the scale and scope of their operations, while at the same time more of these enterprises have begun operation.

Auto-Dialers

One of these technological "advances" has been the use of auto-dialers — devices, usually computer-assisted, that dial telephone numbers automatically — to place the calls. Although auto-dialers, in conjunction with computer systems, have been used to assist humans to place these calls and to increase the productivity of many telemarketing "boiler-room" operations for some time, total automation of the process has become ever more popular in recent times. Typically an auto-dialer dials a number, and upon detecting that the call has been answered, plays a recorded message. Although many of these devices can be programmed with lists of specific numbers, the less sophisticated units simply dial sequential numbers within a range specified by the equipment operator. For this reason, even subscribers with unlisted and carefully guarded telephone numbers are vulnerable to these calls. This has also become a problem in some instances with safety and security lines (e.g., police, fire, ambulance, etc.).

Technology as a Victim

Not only is new technology being used to facilitate the targeting and origination of these unsolicited calls, but the technology has also become the target for these calls in an interesting turnaround of events. As a recent example of this phenomenon, facsimile machine owners have been surprised to discover unsolicited advertising literature arriving on their machines. Not only does this practice tie up the valuable facsimile machine resource, but also costs the machine owner for paper and other supplies. As more and more libraries install facsimile machines, this may pose an increasing problem. Another example pertains to dial-up computer services, such as those sometimes offered by libraries and library automation organizations. Typically, these systems are sufficiently sophisticated to attempt to disconnect after a reasonable period of time if no modem-carrier signal is detected, but many computer-generated calls do not terminate when the called party hangs up. Since many telephone company switches are designed to terminate the call when the calling (originating) party hangs up, the incoming lines of the called system can become congested, causing serious problems.

Still another example involves the rapidly increasing numbers of cellular telephones, which are most often installed in cars, trucks, etc., and in some instances private boats. Cellular subscribers are often annoyed by such unsolicited calls while traveling in their vehicles. Most cellular subscribers pay not only a monthly fee for the service, but also a usage-related fee, usually calculated on the number of minutes of "air time" used. They too often find themselves unable to place a call until the recorded message — sometimes lasting several minutes — plays to completion, while paying for the air time as they wait. This inability to disconnect recorded messages is equally troublesome for PBXs and other affected systems. It should also be noted that in some telephone exchanges where the telephone company equipment does disconnect the circuit, it may be necessary for the recipient of these calls to allow upwards of 25 seconds after hanging up for the telephone company equipment to actually disconnect the call. If the called party picks up the phone before that time has elapsed, the disconnect mechanism must begin anew.

Network Architecture and Operation

In order to understand the impact of these calls on certain other organizations, it is necessary to explore some operational and architectural details of the modern telephone network. Many businesses, libraries, and other organizations have installed private branch exchanges (PBXs) on the owner's premises or campus. Since often the majority of calls both originate and terminate at the local site, they are handled internally by the PBX and never "see" the local telephone network. In addition, local telephone stations (instruments) are typically used only a relatively small percentage (i.e., less than 5% to 10%) of the time, even during busy periods of the day. Therefore, it is only necessary to provide a sufficient number of trunks between the local PBX and the telephone company's central office to accommodate the peak number of simultaneous calls arriving and leaving the local premises.

Direct Inward Dialing

The fact that there are many more local instruments than there are incoming trunks necessitates some mechanism for matching incoming calls with the correct instrument. This cannot be done on a physical-line basis, as is the case with residential subscribers or with Centrex service, which can be thought of as a PBX located at the telephone company central office that serves the remote premises. In bygone days, this function was accomplished by a switchboard attendant. Although attendants still perform this function at some organizations, direct inward dialing (DID) has replaced the manual handling of the majority of these calls in the modern network. In the DID environment, the organization buys a block of telephone numbers from the telephone company. When one of these numbers is called, the telephone company central office switch seizes one of the free trunks going to the subscriber's PBX and passes the number being dialed to the PBX. The PBX then automatically completes the call to the appropriate instrument.

Auto-Dialers and DID Groups

DID groups are typically large blocks of contiguous numbers. Hence, when a sequentially programmed auto-dialer wanders into one of these DID blocks, it can tie up trunk facilities for extended periods of time. In the case where the auto-dialing system has multiple ports (i.e., can place several simultaneous calls), this process can cause very serious problems for the organization receiving these calls, virtually shutting down the premises phone system (or online information system). This nonspecific sequential number dialing practice has also caused obvious problems for hospitals and nursing homes. In addition, some PBX systems route unassigned DID calls (i.e., calls to DID numbers not yet assigned to a specific station) to the attendant station, which can cause the attendant to be tied up with these calls for hours on end.

Auto-Dialers and 800 Service

Another problem of which the author has recently become aware involves a sequential auto-dialing operator who programed his equipment to dial blocks of 800 numbers (toll-free long-distance numbers typically used by businesses and other organizations to assist customers or to take orders without the calling party being billed for the long-distance call). A recent incident of this kind at OCLC not only resulted in the organization's 800 service lines being tied up, but also caused OCLC to pay for the long-distance calls — a situation not dissimilar to the cellular problems described earlier.

Auto-Dialers and Paging Systems

Radio paging systems have also unwittingly become the victims of sequentially programed auto-dialers. These so-called beeper services usually employ a single radio transmitter to relay messages to a large number of subscribers. Making use of a large DID group, these systems typical accept the DID number of the called beeper from the telephone company central office switch and translate this number into a unique code. When transmitted by the radio transmitter, this code activates only the beeper for which the subsequent message is intended, or in some systems simply activates the alarm for that specific subscriber. Many modern paging systems take advantage of digital technology to digitize the received message and record it, along with the associated unique code, on a magnetic disk. This information is then queued for later transmission on the radio transmitter when it becomes available — typically within minutes, even at peak-traffic times.

When a sequentially programed auto-dialer wanders into one of these DID groups, the paging system can be overburdened and the transmitter essentially blocked by large numbers of these calls. Significant delays in transmitting messages can subsequently occur, and literally hundreds of beepers can go off without appropriate cause. Since bona fide messages can be intermixed with the unsolicited calls within the system message queue, it is impossible to remove the unwanted calls en masse from the system without examining each one. This situation is particularly troublesome since these systems are often used by medical and emergency personnel, hospitals, security services, etc., where prompt delivery of the messages is essential. This problem is only exacerbated in the case of national and international radio paging systems that replace the single radio transmitter with large numbers of transmitters located across the country or around the world that are connected to the central system via a network of very expensive terrestrial and/or satellite circuits.

Summary

Fortunately, few libraries or information systems of which the author is aware use paging systems widely, but most use the telephone network to deliver services and carry on their daily operations, either by voice, facsimile, or automated online systems. In addition, many professionals travel in the course of carrying out their professional responsibilities.

The various issues discussed in this chapter have implications for library and information professionals — both in the form of potential opportunities, and as issues and elements of a possibly more problematic nature. It is hoped that this brief overview of these topics will help provide an awareness and background that will help the reader capitalize on any potential benefits, while avoiding potential pitfalls.

"Observe due measure, for right timing is in all things
the most important factor."
(The Theogony) Hesiod [c.700 B.C.]

Future Networking Strategies

As the telecommunications transmission and switching infrastructure evolves toward end-to-end all digital facilities, many feel the historic differentiation between data networks and voice networks will fade and disappear in much the same way as the distinction between computers and telecommunications equipment and techniques is already disappearing. Heretofore, separate data networks were necessary because the analog elements of the switched public network simply did not provide the necessary support for data communications functions, or because of the economics involved in a highly regulated environment where prices more often reflected regulatory policy than underlying cost and market factors. These data networks most often were private networks, using dedicated private-line facilities on an exclusive basis, and nearly always with less efficient utilization of the capabilities of these facilities than is typically the case within the switched public network.

As literally billions of dollars are being expended to digitize and upgrade the switched public network, and as such advanced offerings as integrated services digital network (ISDN) take advantage of these new facilities to plow inroads further and further into the mainstream of the public network, the future of separate and overlapping data and voice networks is being questioned by more and more organizations.

Evolution of LANs

As microprocessor-based workstations have taken their place in offices, libraries, and other organizations, the potential benefits of allowing the various systems to intercommunicate have inevitably been recognized. The first such networks were jokingly called "AdidasNets," based on the way they operated — the operator copied his data file onto a floppy disk, put on his Adidas track shoes, and ran down the hall to the workstation where the data file was needed! It wasn't too long before some workstations — particularly within organizations where the workstations were located in different geographic locations — were equipped with modems and communications software capable of sending and receiving data files over the telephone. The cost of modems, however, generally restricted their use to situations where multiple locations were involved — the floppy-disk network was usually still relied upon within a given location (after all, a five-minute walk with a 360 Kbyte floppy disk represents a 9600 bps communications channel!).

In situations where large amounts of data were routinely exchanged, or where several people within a work group often used the same files (e.g., engineering projects or software system development efforts), a better approach evolved. Through the use of local area network (LAN) technology, the operating systems of the various workstations were integrated in such a way as to communicate and share data effectively over a relatively high-speed local network. These LANs, typically operating at speeds upwards of 10 Mbps, had other advantages as well, often allowing the various workstations to share expensive printing, storage, and other peripheral equipment, and to be linked through gateways to other networks or mainframe computers. It is the local nature, the relatively high speed, and the integration of the operating system and communications technology that typically distinguishes these local area networks.

Where the requirement existed for high-capacity, high-speed communications (e.g., computer-aided design, or CAD, and computer-aided manufacturing, or CAM), such LANs were ideal, and have become a mainstay within the computer/communications industry. However, many applications do not require the high-speed capabilities of these LANs. For these applications, connectivity rather than speed is frequently the goal.

Connectivity

To solve this connectivity problem, usually one of two approaches is taken:

1. An integrated voice/data PBX (private branch exchange; a type of telecommunications switching device usually located at the user's site) that provides both voice and data connectivity for the organization

2. A separate data PBX (sometimes called a data circuit switch, or DCS) that provides the data connectivity in addition to, but separate from, a voice switching capability — either a PBX, or so-called Centrex service offered by the local telephone company. (Centrex can be thought of as a PBX located at the telephone company central office, or CO, used to serve the specific organization on a dedicated basis, although it actually uses the telephone company central office switch in a shared manner with the other subscribers within the local telephone exchange area.)

The choice between the two approaches is usually based on cost factors as well as the individual needs and circumstances surrounding the decision. For example, a company that recently purchased a voice PBX might not be eager to replace it with a more expensive integrated voice/data unit

Public Network Solutions

The local telephone companies, on the other hand, had watched many larger customers purchase PBX equipment — often from someone other than the telephone company — and were not enthusiastic with the prospect of Centrex customers purchasing integrated voice/data switches to meet their combined voice/data needs. Thus the concept of a central-office-based local area network, or CO-LAN, evolved. Among other things, this enabled the telephone company to market a switched data service to its existing Centrex customers. It should be noted that about the only thing a CO-LAN has in common with a LAN — in the generally understood sense of the word, such as the readily available commercial Ethernet or Token Ring LANs — are the letters *LAN* in its name. CO-LANs are functionally much more akin to premises-based data PBXs, providing data connectivity between different work-stations, or terminals/workstations and mainframe computers.

In today's environment, users that require high-speed, high-capacity capabilities have few options other than LANs. This can create a problem, however, when communications between distant locations are required. This has led to various schemes for interconnecting LANs over large distances, and the evolution of specialized networks to meet these requirements (e.g., high-speed research networks used to connect colleges and universities, supercomputer centers, etc.). In the future, however, integrated services digital network (ISDN) — particularly the evolving broadband ISDN, or B-ISDN — holds great promise to provide this functionality more ubiquitously, reliably, and economically.

The Mainframe Approach

It should be noted that another approach to the networking problem, where centralized mainframe systems have been involved, has been to connect terminals/workstations to the mainframe computer and then interconnect the various mainframe computers via specialized networks. This hierarchical approach makes sense only where the functionality of the mainframe computer is required to perform some task that cannot be performed more effectively by the distributed workstation. Presently, large storage requirements or computational requirements that are not well suited, or even possible, on microcomputer-based workstations remain as examples of where this approach makes practical sense. As microcomputer and storage capabilities continue to advance, related costs continue to decrease, and open and distributed architectures continue to evolve, this approach will become less appropriate, as well as less popular. It just makes much more sense to allow the workstation to do what it can, and communicate directly — through a ubiquitous high-capability communications network such as ISDN/B-ISDN — with the computational or file storage resource that might be required to complete the task. It makes little sense to force the communications to occur through intermediate mainframe computer applications where this serves no productive purpose.

A Public or Private Network Solution

Where the lower capability, circuit-switched facilities will suffice, integrated voice/data PBXs, data PBXs, or CO-LAN facilities may currently offer a better solution than LANs. Integrated voice/data switches are typically much more expensive (often four to five times more expensive per port) than data PBXs. Although prices for data PBXs as low as $125 per port are quoted in the literature, the author's experience reflects a per-port cost of about two to three times this number for a fully functional unit when terminal equipment (e.g., short-haul modems), wiring, and other related costs are considered. CO-LAN costs are in the neighborhood of $300 for installation of the terminating equipment (a data-over-voice, or DOV, multi-plexor; technology that allows voice and data to traverse the same telephone line simultaneously) and $20 to $25 per month — somewhat more expensive than a data PBX.

It should be noted that telephone companies use different technologies for provision of CO-LAN service and provide the service under different tariffs or terms, so prices may vary somewhat. Prices and capabilities also change rapidly in the current telecommunications environment, and the purpose here is not to recommend one technology over another — this choice will obviously depend upon numerous user-specific needs and circumstances. Rather, the purpose is to provide an overview of the territory — an understanding of the landscape that will help make several important points.

Viewing the Networking Problem

The networking problem should be viewed in at least four dimensions:

1. The capability of the technology to meet user needs (i.e., a definition and match of user requirements and technology)

2. The ability of the user to install, maintain, and support the networking technology (i.e., is it best for the user to provide the service himself or let someone else provide, manage, and maintain the required service)

3. How both the user needs and the available technology are expected to evolve over time (i.e., the critical time factor in the decision equation)

4. The costs (and benefits) associated with the various solutions when time is considered as a determining parameter in the equation.

In the present environment, the user with high-capacity needs is generally not well served by the switched public network, but with the evolution of ISDN, or B-ISDN, this will likely not remain the case. These needs will most likely be met for the present time using LANs and specialized networks. But in the future, it is unlikely that this will remain an economic solution to the problem. Nevertheless, it is currently necessary for these users to install and support the current solution, or to contract for this function, since it is not generally available, if at all, from the public network.

Users with less demanding requirements do have the choice, in the current environment, of providing the function themselves (e.g., integrated voice/data PBX, or voice PBX and data PBX) or using the public network (e.g., Centrex and CO-LANs). Centrex and CO-LANs may tend to be a bit more "pricey," but this should be expected in light of the added value of these services, particularly when service levels, maintenance, and floor space and other environmental factors such as protection from power outage are considered. The choice includes the option of a private- or a public-network solution.

Today's Strategies for Tomorrow's Network

The critical element today, when making networking decisions, is the time factor. An organization with a good handle on both its evolving needs and evolving potential solutions has a tremendous strategic advantage. If ISDN becomes the networking solution of choice in the future, then it would appear that the best strategic direction would be to evolve toward use of public network solutions. This makes equally good sense for high-capacity needs, since these are expected to be adequately met by the ISDN technologies. The evolution of the Open Network Architecture (ONA) may also provide effective networking solutions within the public network in the interim. The salient questions remain, however, when will ONA and ISDN be available to meet these needs, at what costs, and how will the specific user needs evolve, thus possibly distorting the match between current solutions and future needs.

Time is the critical parameter in planning networking solutions. User needs must be carefully assessed as they are expected to evolve. Technical networking solutions must be selected on the basis, first and foremost, of meeting those needs over time. Investments and financial analyses must take into account, to the fullest extent possible, the changing environment expected over the selected planning horizon. It makes little sense, for example, to jump to Centrex and CO-LANs simply because of an expectation that at some point in the future, public network solutions may be the solutions of choice. There may well be intermediate solutions that will meet the user needs and present far better investment/cost parameters. It makes even less sense, however, to totally ignore the rapidly changing environment and key current networking decisions to only current needs; ignoring the fact that needs as well as opportunities will likely change.

Summary

The public versus private network issue is one that won't go away, and will likely become more prevalent as time passes. This is a major strategic issue. Implementations and investments must be optimized over a planning horizon — most analysts have trouble seeing that time period to be more than three to five years — in such a way as to adequately take into account both the evolving user needs and requirements, as well as the evolving telecommunications infrastructure. It might also be noted that it is not uncommon for a combination of two or three technologies to provide a better solution to the networking problem than any single technology alone. But although this may enhance the effectiveness of the solution, it usually also significantly complicates the decision making process.

Glossary

2B+D. *See* basic rate interface

23B+D. *See* primary rate interface

232 cable. Cable charged to FCC account no. 232 by local telephone companies. This cable was sometimes called grey wire because it was often — but not always — enclosed in a grey covering.

242 cable. Cable charged to FCC account no. 242 by local telephone companies. Riser cable and distribution cable were generally charged to this account in the past. This cable was sometimes called black wire because if was often — but not always — enclosed in a black covering.

800 service. *See* wide area telecommunications service

911 service. *See* enhanced 911 service

950 service. *See* feature group B

access charge. *See* carrier common line charge

ACD. *See* automatic call director

acoustic coupler. A device into which one puts a telephone handset so that information can be transmitted. The device converts digital signals into analog signals, enabling data to be transmitted over the public telephone network via a conventional telephone handset.

adaptive differential pulse code modulation (ADPCM). A common form of speech digitization that transmits at an effective 32 Kbps by encoding the changes between successive samples of the analog waveform, rather than the sample value itself, resulting in about half as much data. *See also* pulse code modulation

address. A coded representation of the destination of data, or of the originating data source.

ADPCM. *See* adaptive differential pulse code modulation

Advanced Research Project Agency Network (ARPANET). In 1968, the Defense Advanced Research Projects Agency (DARPA) embarked on a project to implement a resource sharing network called the ARPA network, or ARPANET. The network was designated to provide effective and efficient communications between heterogeneous computer systems. Operating responsibility for ARPANET was transferred from DARPA to the Defense Communications Agency in July 1975.

aggregate input. The sum of all data rates of the terminals or computer ports connected to a multiplexor or concentrator.

alternating current (AC). Electric current that flows alternately in two directions. *See also* direct current

alternative operator service (AOS). An organization other than AT&T or the several Bell operating companies (BOCs) that provides operator services. These operations often also resell telecommunications service and/or facilities purchased or leased from other telecommunications carriers.

AM. *See* amplitude modulation

American (National) Standard Code for Information Interchange (ASCII). The standard code, using a coded character set consisting of seven-bit coded characters (eight-bits including parity check), used for information interchange among data-processing systems, data-communications systems, and associated equipment.

American National Standards Institute (ANSI). The principal standards development body in the United States. ANSI was formed in 1918 and evolved through several forms until 1969. ANSI is a nonprofit, nongovernmental organization supported by more than 1,000 trade organizations, professional societies and companies. It serves as the national clearinghouse for voluntary standards and is America's representative body before the International Standards Organization (ISO).

amplification. The strengthening of an electrical signal by means of an amplifier.

amplifier. A device used to strengthen an electrical signal.

amplitude modulation (AM). One of three ways of modifying a sine wave, or carrier, to make it carry information. The carrier sine wave has its amplitude modified in accordance with the information to be transmitted.

analog circuit. A data-communications channel on which the information can take any value between the limits defined by the channel. *See also* digital circuit

analog signal. A signal that can take any value between the limits defined by the channel. Such signals are analogous to the information signal being transmitted. *See also* digital signal

ANSI. *See* American National Standards Institute

AOS. *See* Alternative operator service

ARPANET. *See* Advanced Research Project Agency Network

ASCII. *See* American standard code for information interchange

asynchronous transmission. Transmission in which time intervals between transmitted characters may be of unequal length. Transmission is controlled by start and stop bits at the beginning and end of each character. No additional synchronizing or timing information need be transmitted. Also called start-stop transmission. *See also* synchronous transmission

attenuation. The difference between transmitted and received signal power due to loss through transmission facilities and devices. The decrease in magnitude of a signal.

auto-answer. A modem feature that detects an incoming call and responds to it by returning an answer tone.

auto-dial. A modem feature that allows a computer user to place a call without having to dial a number. A computer equipped with an auto-dial modem takes a phone number stored in its memory, instructs the modem to dial the number, and waits for an answer tone from the computer being called. When the modem receives this tone, it responds with an originate tone, completing the connection.

automatic call director (ACD). A device used to answer incoming telephone calls and direct them to one of several attendants. These devices are typically used to queue calls for service attendants on a next available (or some other) basis, or to direct calls to specific attendants or groups of attendants by requesting the caller to indicate the target by touching a particular key on a dual-tone multifrequency (DTMF), or Touch-Tone, phone.

backbone circuit. *See* interlocation trunking

backbone trunk. *See* interlocation trunking

back-hauled call. A call, usually long distance, intercepted and carried to a remote operations center by a carrier — usually an alternative operator service, where it is subsequently routed to its destination, often using the long-distance facilities of another carrier. The first leg of such back-hauled calls is usually transparent to both the caller and the subsequent carrier, and can give rise to elements of confusion when the caller is subsequently billed for the call.

B-channel. The basic building block of the ISDN is the 64 Kbps B-channel. The B-channel may be used for voice and circuit- or packet-switched data.

balanced line. A transmission line consisting of two conductors in which the sum of the electrical currents is always zero. Equal and opposite currents flowing in the separate conductors are used to convey the information being transmitted.

bandpass. *See* bandwidth

band splitter. A multiplexor designed to split the available bandwidth into several independent narrower band subchannels, each suitable for data transmission at a fraction of the total channel data rate.

bandwidth. Denotes the range of frequencies a channel is capable of transmitting. The difference between the highest and lowest frequencies in a band, such as 3000 Hz bandwidth in a voice grade line (i.e., 3300–300 Hz).

baseband. A bandpass utilization technique wherein the entire bandpass is shared on the basis of time with a single transmission taking place at any given time. The technique, which is a form of time-division multiplexing, is often used in local area networks. *See also* broadband

basic exchange telephone radio (BETR). A radio-based mechanism for accessing the local telephone company central office. BETR is most frequently used in rural areas where construction of terrestrial access circuits is more costly.

basic rate interface (BRI). The interface used to connect telephones, terminals, PCs and other desktop devices to higher-order equipment and to the network. The BRI includes two 64 Kbps B-channels and one 16 Kbps D-channel. The BRI is used with integrated services digital network (ISDN BRI is synonymous with 2B+D).

basic service. The common carrier offering of transmission capacity for the movement of information between two or more points. Under provisions of the FCC Computer Inquiry II, basic service is offered under tariff by AT&T and the BOCs. *See also* enhanced service

basic service element (BSE). As a result of computer inquiry III and the FCC-mandated open network architecture, a variety of network services must be made available by the local exchange company on an unbundled basis to enhanced service providers. These services are called basic service elements. *See also* basic serving arrangement

basic serving arrangement (BSA). As a result of computer inquiry III and the FCC-mandated open network architecture, various facilities, called basic serving arrangements, that provide access to basic service elements, must be made available by the local exchange company, on an unbundled basis, to enhanced service providers.

basket (a.k.a. market basket). A regulatory concept wherein prices for a class of services (i.e., a basket) are regulated in the aggregate, rather than on an individual service basis.

baud. A unit of signaling speed equal to the number of discrete conditions or signal elements per second. Since a signal element may contain more than one bit, one baud may be, but is not necessarily, equal to one bit per second (bps). *See also* bit per second

baudot code. A code for the transmission of data in which five equal-length bits represent one character. This code is used in some teletypewriter machines where one start element and one stop element (used for timing or synchronization) are added.

BCC. *See* block check character

bel. A control character that is used when there is a need to call for attention; it may control alarm or attention devices.

Bell operating company (BOC). One of the 22 local exchange carriers divested by AT&T under terms of the Modified Final Judgment. The 22 BOCs are now individually held by one of the seven regional Bell holding companies.

Bell System. AT&T and the 22 local Bell operating companies prior to Divestiture. Also, the network and infrastructure owned, maintained, and operated by the AT&T and the 22 Bell operating companies prior to Divestiture.

Bernoulli Box. The Bernoulli Box is a cross between a hard disk and a floppy disk that uses a cushion of air instead of a motor to move the disk around. With flexible, removable cartridges, it provides the mass storage of a hard disk without the attendant problems of head crashes or permanent inclusion of the disk in the drive unit.

BETR. *See* basic exchange telephone radio

binary digit (bit). In binary notation, either of the characters *0* or *1*. An information element assigned one of two possibilities.

bisync. An acronym (binary synchronous) for an IBM communications protocol. It uses a defined set of control characters and control character sequences for synchronized transmission of binary coded data between stations in a data communications system.

bisynchronous transmission (BSC). *See* bisync

bit. *See* binary digit

bit per second (bps). A unit of signaling speed equal to the number of binary digits (bits) per second. *See also* baud

bit rate. The speed at which bits are transmitted, usually expressed in bits per second (bps). *See also* baud

black cable (a.k.a. black wire). *See* 242 cable

block. A group of bits or characters transmitted as a unit. An encoding procedure generally is applied to the group for error detection and/or correction purposes.

block check character (BCC). The result of a transmission verification algorithm accumulated over a transmission block, and normally appended at the end. *See also* cyclic redundancy check, or CRC; vertical redundancy check, or VRC; and longitudinal redundancy check, or LRC

BOC. *See* Bell operating company

bong tone. A distinctive electronic gong-like tone generated by some telephone switches, and used to signify to a caller placing a 0-plus call that the caller should dial a credit-card number.

bps. *See* bit per second

BRI. *See* basic rate interface

broadband. A bandpass utilization technique wherein the available spectrum of frequencies is divided into several channels, each of which is capable of simultaneous communications. The technique, which is a form of frequency-division multiplexing, is often used in local area networks. *See also* baseband

BRS. Information service [BRS, 1200 Route 7, Latham, New York 12110, (518)-783-1161].

BSC. *See* bisynch

buffer. Computer memory in which data are temporarily held in anticipation of processing or transmission. In telecommunications, such data are typically held to facilitate synchronization, switching or redirecting, or retransmission in case of error.

Bundled services. Various telecommunications services that are offered by a provider (usually a regulated common carrier) only as a package, wherein the constituent services are not made available on an individual basis.

bus. One or more conductors used for transmitting signals, data, or power. Often a bus acts as a common connection between several locations.

bypass. The transmission of long-distance messages that do not use the facilities of local telephone companies available to the general public, but that could use such facilities.

byte. A binary element string operated upon as a unit and usually shorter than a computer word. Eight-bit bytes are most common. Byte is often used interchangeably with character.

call store function. The capability, usually provided within a PBX, central office switch, or by an attached adjunct device, to record and maintain information about calls placed and/or received. Information typically includes origination telephone station number, time and duration of the call, called station number, and other facilities-related information.

carriage return (CR). A format effector which moves the active position to the first character position of the same line.

carrier. *See* carrier signal; *see also* common carrier

carrier common line charge (CCLC). A fee which the FCC ordered paid to the local telephone company by the interexchange carriers based on their use of the local network to originate and terminate long-distance traffic to offset the revenue shortfall that resulted from the breakup of the Bell system and the subsequent loss of cross subsidies from long-distance services. It should be noted that these charges were designed to recover fixed, or so-called nontraffic sensitive (NTS) costs, but were actually assessed on the basis of minutes-of-use by the IXC as a mechanism of prorating the fees among the various interexchange network providers.

carrier frequency. The frequency, most frequently the center or average frequency, of a carrier signal.

carrier signal. An electronic signal upon which information is imposed for the purpose of transmission. The carrier signal is said to be modulated during this process. Carrier signals are generally used to move the transmission of information to a frequency band more readily accommodated by the transmission medium. *See also* common carrier

CCITT. *See* International Consultative Committee for Telegraphy and Telephony

CCLC. *See* carrier common line charge

CCS. *See* common channel signaling

CEI. *See* comparably efficient interconnection

cellular radio. A radio telecommunications scheme wherein a geographic area is divided into cells, each with a centrally located antenna, and a mobile unit is passed from cell to cell in a manner transparent to the mobile user as cell boundaries are crossed. Radio frequencies are reused within the various cells, thus making more efficient use of the limited spectrum of available frequencies.

central office (CO). The place where communications common carriers terminate customer lines and locate the switching equipment that interconnects those lines.

central office-based local area network (CO-LAN). Data switching capabilities provided by telephone company central office switching equipment. Although the name might imply functionality similar to that offered by local area networks, CO-LAN functionality is more closely related to that provided by a data PBX.

central office switch. The switching equipment located at a telephone company central office.

central processing unit (CPU). A unit of a computer that includes circuits controlling the interpretation and execution of instructions.

Centrex. A telecommunications offering that utilizes the capabilities of the telephone company central office switch to provide telephone service similar to the capabilities provided by a private branch exchange.

Centrex console. The operator attendant station and related equipment, typically located at the customer location and used to support Centrex service.

channel attached device. A peripheral device directly connected to the input/output mechanism (called a channel) of a computer.

channel bank. Channel terminal equipment used for combining (multiplexing) channels on a frequency-division or time-division basis. Equipment for transmitting more than one voice channel over a wideband path by sampling the speech, coding the sample, and using digital techniques.

channel capacity. A term that expresses the maximum data rate that can be handled by a communications channel.

channel service unit (CSU). An access arrangement used with digital data channels (e.g., Dataphone Digital Service) that provides local-loop equalization, transient protection, isolation and central office loopback testing capability.

character. A representation consisting of a fixed number of bits. Most commonly 7 bits (e.g., ASCII) or 8 bits (e.g., EBCDIC).

circuit switch. A device used to establish, maintain, and terminate a telecommunications connection. Circuit switches are distinguished from other types of telecommunications switches in that the established circuit is maintained for the user on a dedicated bases for the duration of the call.

clear to send (CTS). The physical modem interface control signal from data communication equipment (DCE) that indicates to the data terminal equipment (DTE) that it may begin data transmission.

clock. A shorthand term for the source(s) of timing signals used in synchronous transmission. More generally, the source(s) of timing signals sequencing electronic events.

cluster. A term used to describe a terminal configuration in which two or more terminals are connected to a single line or single modem.

CO. *See* central office

CO-LAN. *See* central-office-based local area network

collocate. A regulatory concept that allows organizations other than the telephone company, typically an enhanced service provider, to locate network equipment within the central office of the respective telephone company. This provides for ready and effective interconnection of the customer equipment to the telephone network.

common carrier. A supplier that provides telecommunications transmission capabilities using a telecommunications network to the public or certain segments of the public.

Common Carrier Bureau (the Bureau). The bureau within the FCC which is responsible for regulation of telecommunications.

common channel signaling (CCS). Communication of call signaling information using a communications channel different from the channel that carries the call itself.

Communications Act of 1934 (the Act). This Act, passed by Congress in 1934, established a national telecommunications goal of high-grade, universally available telephone service at reasonable cost. The Act also established the FCC and transferred federal regulation of all interstate and foreign wire and radio communications to this commission.

communications protocol. The means used to control the orderly communication of information between stations on a data link. A formal set of conventions governing the format and relative timing of message exchange between two computers.

comparably efficient interconnection (CEI). The name given to the specific case-by-case application of the more general open network architecture requirements. Prior to approval of the more general open network architecture plans of the various carriers by the FCC, a carrier would be allowed to provide certain enhanced services subject to nonstructural safeguards, on the basis of a case-by-case review and approval.

compensation. *See* conditioning

competitive service. A telecommunications service area in which sufficient competition is perceived to exist so that competitive constraints by government regulation on dominant common carriers are not required.

complex cable. The telecommunications cables, including associated components and necessary conduit, that connect telecommunications equipment shared by multiple users with telephones, terminals, and other related equipment usually located within the same building or in buildings on contiguous property.

composite link. The line or circuit connecting a pair of multiplexors or concentrators; the circuit carrying multiplexed data.

CompuServe. Information service [CompuServe, Inc., 5000 Arlington Centre Boulevard, Columbus, Ohio 43220, (614) 457-8600].

Computer Inquiry I (CI-I). A five-year inquiry begun in 1966 by the FCC that ended in 1971 with a ruling that (with minor exceptions) common carriers could provide data processing services to entities other than themselves through completely separate affiliates.

Computer Inquiry II (CI-II). A four-year inquiry begun in 1976 by the FCC that resulted in a ruling that, effective January 1, 1982, it would no longer attempt to define data processing separately from data communications, and established two new classes of services: basic and enhanced.

Computer Inquiry III (CI-III). An inquiry begun in 1986 by the FCC that resulted in a proposal to substitute nonstructural safeguards for existing computer inquiry II subsidiary rules.

concentrator. *See* statistical multiplexor

conditioning. Analog waveforms are frequently distorted in magnitude and propagation speed as the frequency varies during transmission over telecommunications channels. This distortion is often of an arbitrary, but mostly consistent nature for a given channel. Conditioning is accomplished by deliberately applying an additional distortion using electrical techniques in such a way as to counteract the channel-produced distortion and reproduce a signal near to the original waveform to be presented to the terminal equipment.

contamination. Intrastate telecommunications facilities that carry some elements of interstate traffic are said to be contaminated, and hence subject to federal jurisdiction.

contention. A condition on a communications channel when two or more stations try to transmit at the same time. The process of bidding for a communications channel by multiple users.

core restrictions. Restrictions set forth in the Modified Final Judgment (MFJ), or Divestiture agreement, prohibiting the BOCs from participating in the long-distance, information services, or equipment manufacturing markets.

cost-based pricing. A regulatory concept wherein the price for a regulated service is based on the cost to provide that service.

CPE. *See* customer premises equipment

CPU. *See* central processing unit

CR. *See* carriage return

CRC. *See* cyclic redundancy check

cross-subsidization. The process of using excess revenue derived from one service or market area in order to offer service at less than cost in another area. This process can result in noncompetitive prices when the excess revenues are derived from monopoly service areas.

crosstalk. The unwanted transfer of energy from one circuit, called the disturbing circuit, to another circuit, called the disturbed circuit. A type of telecommunications interference.

CTS. *See* clear to send

current loop. A method of interconnecting terminals and transmitting signals, whereby a mark (i.e., binary 1) is represented by current on the line and a space (i.e., binary 0) is represented by the absence of current on the line.

customer premises equipment (CPE). All telecommunications terminal equipment located on the customer's premises. At one time, this equipment was required to be provided by the telephone company. Subsequently, AT&T and the RBOCs were required to provide CPE through separate subsidiaries (i.e., not by the regulated company) in competition with other suppliers. Some telecommunications equipment located on the customer's premises was, however, classified as transmission equipment, and was offered by the regulated companies. Currently, regulated companies can offer CPE, but must keep track of these business activities separately from their regulated business.

cyclic redundancy check (CRC). An error detection scheme in which the check character is generated by taking the remainder after dividing all the serialized bits in a block by a predetermined polynomial.

D-channel. A key characteristic of ISDN is its ability to carry bandwidth outside of information channels. This allows the exchange of control information between the user and the network. Such control information is required to set up calls between users, redirect calls, change their properties and terminate calls. The D-channel is called an out-of-band signaling channel.

DAA. *See* data access arrangement

DARPA. *See* Defense Advanced Research Projects Agency

data access arrangement. Data communications equipment furnished or approved by a common carrier permitting attachment of privately owned data terminal and data communications equipment to the common carrier network, normally the dial network. It is no longer necessary to utilize a DAA provided the equipment to be attached to the public network meets certain standard requirements and has received FCC certification.

database service. An enhanced service provider that offers access to one or more computer databases. Also, the service offered by such a provider.

data communications equipment (DCE). The equipment that provides the functions required to establish, maintain, and terminate a data transmission connection (e.g., a modem).

data PBX. A private branch exchange that is used to provide data, rather than voice, switching services. These devices typically provide point-to-point data connections at up to 64 Kbps, and are generally used to interconnect terminals, workstations, and host computers within a single location or campus. *See also* local area network

Dataphone Digital Service (DDS). A communications service offering in which data are transmitted in digital rather than analog form, thus eliminating the need for modems.

data set ready (DSR). The physical modem interface control signal from the data communications equipment (DCE) which indicates to the attached terminal equipment that the modem is connected to the telephone circuit.

data terminal equipment (DTE). The equipment acting as data source, data sink, or both (e.g., telephone set, terminal or computer).

data terminal ready (DTR). The physical modem interface control signal from the data terminal device indicating to the modem that the terminal is ready for transmission.

DC. *See* direct current

DCE. *See* data communications equipment

DDD. *See* direct distance dialing

DDS. *See* Dataphone Digital Service

dedicated line. A telephone line used exclusively by one customer. The line usually does not pass through public network switching equipment, and is provided for a monthly service charge independent of the amount of use on the line. *See also* dial-up line

Defense Advanced Research Projects Agency (DARPA). A separately organized agency within the United States Department of Defense under a director appointed by the Secretary of Defense. The agency engages in advanced basic and applied research and development projects essential to the Department of Defense. It also conducts prototype projects that embody technology that may be incorporated into joint programs, programs in support of deployed United States forces or selected military department programs, and, on request, assists the military departments in their prototype efforts.

DEMS. *See* digital electronic message services

demultiplexing. A process for separating into individual channels a common bit stream or common frequency band which has been multiplexed. *See also* multiplexing

demultiplexor. A device that performs demultiplexing.

depreciation cost surplus. The difference between the current value and the book value, as reflected from the regulatory process, of telephone company equipment. This represents an accumulated cost which must be amortized by the local telephone company as network modernization occurs.

DIALOG. Information service [DIALOG Information Services, Inc., 3460 Hillview Avenue, Palo Alto, California 94304, (415)-858-3785].

dial-up line. A communications circuit that is established by a switched-circuit, using the public dial telephone network.

dibit. A group of two bits. The four possible states for a dibit code are 00, 01, 10, and 11. Often modems encode more than one bit in each signal element transmitted (e.g., dibits when two bits are so encoded).

DID. *See* Direct Inward Dialing

differential phase shift keying (DPSK). The modulation technique used in the Bell 201 modem. A modulation technique wherein the phase of the carrier signal is abruptly modified.

digital circuit. A data-communications channel designed specifically to handle digital signals. *See also* analog circuit

digital electronic message services (DEMS). The FCC classification for services under which microwave spectrum for digital termination system is allocated. *See also* digital termination system

digital signal. A digital signal is a discrete or discontinuous signal; one whose various states are discrete intervals apart. *See also* analog circuit

digital termination system (DTS). A microwave system used to broadcast from a central local location to many low-cost receivers on various users' roofs, etc. DTS uses radio-packet techniques in order to share the facility in an effective manner.

direct current (DC). Electric current that flows in only one direction. *See also* alternating current

direct distance dialing (DDD). A method of making toll telephone calls on the public-switched telephone network without the aid of an operator.

Direct Inward Dialing (DID). The ability to directly reach a called station without the necessity to first go through a switchboard attendant. Also, the capability for a PBX, or other remote switching device, to accept called station identification information from a central office switch over a common trunk facility and complete the call to the called station without operator attendant intervention.

Direct Outward Dialing (DOD). The ability to place a call on the public network without the necessity of obtaining an outside line from an operator attendant. Also, the capability for a PBX, or other remote switching device, to place calls on the public network without the necessity of operator attendant intervention.

discriminatory pricing. A regulatory concept wherein a specific regulated service is provided to different subscribers at substantially different prices. Discriminatory pricing is explicitly prohibited by the Communications Act of 1934.

distributed architecture. A system architecture in which processing functions are moved from a central computer to remotely located computers or terminals.

distributed processing. *See* distributed architecture

distributed switching. A telecommunications switching arrangement wherein the switching functions are moved from a central switch to remote local switches.

distribution cable. Telecommunications wiring used to connect different telephone closets within a building or campus.

Divestiture. In 1974, the United States Department of Justice brought an antitrust action against AT&T seeking to dismantle the Bell system. In January of 1982, AT&T signed a consent decree, which became known as the Modified Final Judgment or Divestiture agreement, agreeing to divest itself of the local portions of its 22 local operating companies (BOCs). This process has become known as Divestiture.

DMS-100. *See* electronic switching system

DOD. *See* direct outward dialing

domestic satellite carrier (DSC). An intercity carrier which provides communications services within the United States via a domestic satellite.

dominant common carrier. A carrier having control over a substantial portion or subportion of the telecommunications market. FCC Docket 79-252 defines a dominant carrier as one having significant market power. This includes AT&T and the BOCs in the voice telecommunications market.

DPSK. *See* differential phase shift keying

DSC. *See* domestic satellite carrier

DSR. *See* data set ready

DTE. *See* data terminal equipment

DTMF. *See* dual-tone multifrequency

DTR. *See* data terminal ready

DTS. *See* digital termination system

dual-tone multifrequency (DTMF). A telecommunication signaling format that represents the digits zero through nine, *, and # as unique combinations of two each of five audio frequency tones. This system is also known as Touch-Tone.

E911. *See* enhanced 911 service

echoplex. A method of checking data transmission accuracy whereby the received data characters are returned to the sending end for comparison with the original data.

echo suppressor. An electronic device inserted in a circuit that effectively blocks passage of reflected signals, hence eliminating echoes on the telecommunications circuit.

economy of scale. A principle of economics that provides for decreasing per-unit costs as volume of production, relative organizational or operational size, etc., increases. Typically this results from a relatively fixed overhead being amortized over increasing numbers of units.

EIA. *See* Electronic Industries Association

electrical transient. A momentary aberration or disruption of an electrical signal. Such voltage spikes, electrical current surges, or other aberrations can result in momentary loss of integrity of electrical signals, or in some instances, serious damage to electrical or electronic devices.

Electronic Industries Association (EIA). An American standards organization specializing in the electrical and functional characteristics of interface equipment.

electronic mail. A service wherein text messages are electronically exchanged, typically using store and forward messaging techniques, between terminal or computer workstation devices.

electronic switching system (ESS). A class of modern telecommunications switching systems in which the control functions are performed principally by electronic devices. Devices with various capabilities are manufactured by different manufacturers, and appear with different designations, for example, 1ESS, 2ESS, 4ESS, 5ESS, 1AESS, DMS-100, etc.

EM. *See* end of medium

end of medium (EM). A control character that may be used to identify the physical end, used amount, or wanted portion of data recorded on a medium.

end of text (ETX). A transmission control character which terminates a text.

end of transmission (EOT). A transmission control character used to indicate the conclusion of the transmission of one or more texts.

ENFIA. *See* exchange network facilities for interstate access

enhanced service. A telecommunications service which functions as more than simply a transmission or basic service. Enhanced service is usually associated with the use of computers to add additional function to basic service. Under terms of FCC Computer Inquiry II, enhanced service must be offered by independent subsidiaries of AT&T and the BOCs whose activities, while subject to regulation are not subject to tariffing. With the advent of FCC Computer Inquiry III, enhanced service may be offered by regulated carriers, but this business must be taken into account separately from their regulated business.

enhanced service provider (ESP). Provider of services offered over transmission facilities that utilize computer-based processing applications to provide the subscriber with additional or restructured information.

enhanced 911 service (E911). An emergency service that provides information from the network regarding the identity and location of a calling party to emergency service operators.

ENQ. *See* enquiry

enquiry (ENQ). A transmission control character used as a request for a response from a remote station.

entrance cable. Telephone company cable that provides service to a building or complex. This cable connects the public network to the minimum point of termination.

EOT. *See* end of transmission

equal access. A provision of the Modified Final Judgment or Divestiture which requires the Bell operating companies (BOCs) to provide all interexchange carriers with exchange access services equal in type, quality, and price to those provided to AT&T by September 1, 1986.

equalization. Introduction of controlled distortion into a communications channel at the receiving end in such a manner as to cancel or offset unwanted distortion that has already occurred in the channel.

ESC. *See* escape character

escape character (ESC). A control character which is used to provide additional control functions. It alters the meaning of a limited number of continuously following bit combinations.

ESP. *See* enhanced service provider

ESS. *See* electronic switching system

ET. *See* exchange termination

ETB. *See* end of transmission block

ether. A medium that in the undulatory theory of light permeates all space and transmits transverse waves. This theory, now known to be incorrect, has been superseded by the electromagnetic theory.

ETX. *See* end of text

exchange access services. Services provided by the BOCs that allow interLATA networks provided by interexchange carriers to access customers within a LATA and allow end-users to access interLATA services. Examples of interLATA services might include interLATA and international telephone service and interLATA operator services.

exchange area. Prior to Divestiture, an area within which there was a single uniform set of charges for telephone service. The MFJ defines exchange area or exchange to be generally equivalent to a Standard Metropolitan Statistical Area (SMSA), which is a geographic area defined by the United States government for statistical purposes, called a Local Access and Transport Area (LATA).

exchange network facilities. Transmission facilities within an exchange area used for loops, trunks, and special-service circuits.

exchange network facilities for interstate access (ENFIA). An interstate tariff offering access to exchange network facilities to complete OCCs' public switched voice message interstate services, when such OCCs are duly authorized by the FCC to furnish end-to-end public switched interstate service.

exchange termination (ET). The central office link with an integrated services digital network (ISDN) user.

facsimile. The transmission and reproduction of graphic matter by electrical means. The term is generally applied to transmission of textual material when such transmission is accomplished by treating the text as graphic matter rather than encoded text.

FCC. *See* Federal Communications Commission

FDDI. *See* fiber distributed data interface

FDM. *See* frequency-division multiplexing

feature group A (FGA). Under equal access, a line-side connection to the LEC switch. When FGA is used to connect to a long-distance network, it is usually necessary to dial a seven-to-ten digit access number, followed by an access code, and then the seven-to-ten digit number of the station being called. It is also usually necessary that, with the exception of the access number, the remaining numbers must be dialed with a dual-tone multifrequency (DTMF) or touch-tone instrument.

feature group B (FGB). Under equal access, a trunk-side connection to the LEC switch. When FGB is used to connect to a long-distance network, it is necessary to dial a five-digit number of the form *950-10XX*, where the *XX* is a two-digit number identifying the long-distance carrier that is being requested to carry the call.

feature group C (FGC). Under equal access, the trunk-side connection to the LEC switch that was provided to AT&T prior to Divestiture, and is available to AT&T only, on an interim basis, until FGD can be made available.

feature group D (FGD). A new trunk-side interconnection arrangement designed to meet the equal access requirements of the Divestiture agreement. When a long-distance carrier subscribes to FGD access, subscribers can presubscribe to the services of the specific carrier, whereafter the LEC routes long-distance traffic to this carrier when the subscriber dials *1* plus the long-distance number.

Federal Communications Commission (FCC; the Commission). A board of commissioners, appointed by the President of the United States under the Communications Act of 1934, having the power to regulate interstate and foreign communications originating in the United States by wire and radio.

Federal-State Joint Board. A body established by the FCC to deal with matters (especially financial and regulatory) which affect state interests.

FF. *See* form feed character

fiber distributed data interface (FDDI). An evolving ANSI standard derived from the IEEE 802.5 Token-Ring protocol. FDDI is a 100 Mbps token ring that uses an optical-fiber medium, and proposes a primary and secondary ring.

fiber optics (FO). The branch of optical technology concerned with the transmission of radiant power through fibers made of transparent materials, such as glass, fused silica or plastic. Communications applications employ flexible fibers.

file separator (FS). A control character used to separate and qualify data logically; normally delimits a data item called a file.

FM. *See* frequency modulation

foreign exchange (FX) line. A telecommunications channel connected directly to a remote telephone exchange from a location not contained in that local telephone exchange. For example, a Chicago subscriber might obtain a local New York City phone line via an FX line.

form feed character (FF). A format effector which advances the active position to the same character position on a predetermined line on the next form or page.

four-wire circuit. A telecommunications circuit consisting of two 2-wire circuits. Each two-wire loop is generally used to conduct signals in one direction only — the combination carrying signals in both directions.

frequency-division multiplexing (FDM). A technique for multiplexing a telecommunications channel wherein the available spectrum of frequencies (bandwidth) is divided into two or more contiguous bands of frequencies, usually separated by a small band of frequencies called a guardband; each is utilized simultaneously for independent transmission of information. *See also* time-division multiplexing

frequency modulation (FM). One of three ways of modifying a sine wave signal to make it carry information. The sine wave or carrier has its frequency modified in accordance with the information to be transmitted.

frequency shift keying (FSK). A method of frequency modulation in which frequency is made to vary at significant instants by smooth as well as abrupt transitions. Typically a data 1 is represented as one frequency and a data 0 bit as another frequency. Also called frequency shift signaling.

FS. *See* file separator

FSK. *See* frequency shift keying

full-duplex. Simultaneous, two-way, independent transmission in both directions.

FX. *See* foreign exchange line.

gateway city. One of several cities designated to terminate international telecommunications channels. International segments of telecommunications channels originate or terminate in gateway cities.

Gbps. *See* gigabits per second.

GHz. *See* gigaHertz

gigabits per second. One billion bits per second.

gigaHertz. One billion Hertz, or one billion cycles per second.

grey cable (a.k.a. grey wire). *See* 232 cable

gross national product (GNP) price deflator. An average of the indexes of prices of all the goods and services that make up the GNP weighted by the constant-dollar composition of the GNP in the current period. Thus, changes in the implicit price deflator reflect not only changes in prices but also any shift in the composition of the GNP.

gross national product (GNP) price index. In contrast to the GNP price deflator, the GNP price index is weighted by the composition of the GNP at a fixed point selected as the base period. Such indexes measure the changes in the price of a fixed market basket; thus, they measure only price change.

group separator (GS). A control character used to separate and qualify data logically; normally delimits a data item called a group.

GS. *See* group separator

gypsy calling. When a subscriber, who has presubscribed to a specific long-distance carrier, instructs the LEC switch to route a specific call to another long-distance carrier by dialing *10XXX*, where *XXX* is the carrier identification number of the other carrier. This other carrier must have purchased FGD access to the LEC switch.

half-duplex. Transmission in either direction, but not both directions simultaneously.

handshaking. Exchange of predetermined signals between two devices for purposes of control.

HDLC. *See* high-level data link control

header. The control information prefixed in a message text (e.g., source or destination address, sequence number or message length or type).

Hertz (Hz). The number of cycles per second.

high-level data link control (HDLC). The international standard link-level communications protocol defined by ISO.

Hi-Lo tariff. A two-level rate schedule for AT&T's intercity voice grade private-line service. Under the Hi-Lo rate approach, costs and rates were averaged separately for high-density routes and low-density routes; thus, rates on high-density routes were lower than for low-density routes. In 1976, the FCC declared the Hi-Lo tariff unjustified.

horizontal tab (HT). A format effector which advances the active position to the next predetermined character position on the same line.

HT. *See* horizontal tab

Hz. *See* Hertz

inside wire. Telecommunications wire contained within the customer's premises. Generally, the wire owned and maintained by the customer.

integrated services digital network (ISDN). A public end-to-end digital telecommunications network capable of supporting a wide spectrum of present and emerging user needs such as voice, telemetry, security monitoring, electronic mail, electronic funds transfer, computer inquiry and response, facsimile, computer bulk data transfer, and video.

intelligent building. A building that controls its internal systems. Intelligent buildings often integrate numerous business functions and electronic office services, typically under the control of a digital PBX, a separate computer, or linked computers — often mini- or microcomputers.

intelligent gateway. A device capable of manipulating and/or processing information which is utilized to enable devices on two or more distinct telecommunications networks to communicate. In Library and Information Science, the term is often used to denote devices which provide such services as directories, presearch and/or postsearch processing and/or storage, in addition to the communications functions.

intelligent workstation. A workstation device having substantial processing capabilities. Usually applied to microcomputer-based workstations.

intent. A regulatory concept wherein the intended destination of communication rather than the physical topology of connecting circuits is used to establish jurisdictional authority. An example is three computers in two different states, interconnected in a serial manner by private leased telephone lines. In this case the circuit connecting the two computers within the single state, and solely contained within that state, might be considered to fall under interstate jurisdiction if the messages exchanged were routinely intended for the computer residing within the second state.

interconnect. The direct electrical connection, acoustical coupling, or inductive coupling of customer premises equipment (CPE) to the telephone network. It also includes the direct electrical connection of other common carrier (OCC) facilities to the telephone network.

interexchange carrier (IXC). A common carrier which is authorized to carry information using telecommunications techniques between exchange areas.

interexchange channel (IXC). A telecommunications channel connecting two different exchange areas.

interexchange service. Telecommunication service between exchange areas.

interface coupler. *See* data access arrangement

interlocation trunking. Telecommunications channels connecting telephone switching equipment at two or more different locations.

International Consultative Committee for Telegraphy and Telephony (CCITT). An advisory committee established under the United Nations within the International Telecommunications Union (ITU) to recommend worldwide standards.

International Standards Organization (ISO). An organization established to promote the development of standards to facilitate the international exchange of goods and services, and to develop mutual cooperation in areas of intellectual, scientific, technological, and economic activity.

ISDN. *See* integrated services digital network

ISO. *See* International Standards Organization

IXC. *See* interexchange carrier; interexchange channel

joint access costs. Costs associated with those parts of the telephone network which are used both for local and long-distance calling.

Kbps. *See* kilobit per second

keyboard send/receive (KSR). A combination teleprinter transmitter and receiver with transmission capability from the keyboard only.

key telephone system. A telephone switching system, usually located at a single subscriber location, that is used to answer and complete incoming calls, or to place calls, by means of manual button(s) on one or more of the respective telephone instruments. These systems are typically small systems, and unlike larger and more sophisticated private branch exchanges, are generally used to switch calls among individual telephone subscriber lines, and not to consolidate traffic onto a trunk or group of trunks interconnecting the equipment with the telephone company central office.

KHz. *See* kiloHertz

kilobit per second (Kbps). 1000 bits per second.

kiloHertz (KHz). 1000 Hertz, or 1000 cycles per second.

KSR. *See* keyboard send/receive

LAPB. *See* link access procedure balanced

LAPD (Link access procedure for the D-channel). *See* Q.921

LADT. *See* local area data transport

LAN. *See* local area network

LATA. *See* local access and transport area

leaky PBX. A device, usually a PBX, which allows interstate traffic that is not carried by a public interexchange network to utilize the local switched telephone network. A device that leaks traffic from a private interstate network onto the local public switched telephone network, or vice versa. Such leaked traffic avoids certain network access charges.

leased line. *See* private line

LEC. *See* local exchange carrier

LED. *See* light emitting diode

LF. *See* line feed character

LIDB. *See* line information database

light emitting diode (LED). A semiconductor light source that emits visible or invisible infrared radiation.

line driver. A signal converter which conditions a digital signal to ensure reliable transmission over an extended distance.

line extender. *See* line driver

line feed character (LF). A format effector which advances the active position to the same character position of the next line.

line information database (LIDB). A proposed system wherein the LEC would access a computerized network to ascertain what long-distance carrier a credit-card holder had chosen and route credit-card calls to the carrier designated by the credit-card holder rather than the long-distance carrier to which the calling line had been presubscribed.

line of business (LOB) waiver. The Modified Final Judgment or Divestiture agreement provides that BOCs may provide products or services in addition to exchange and exchange access services, with permission of the court, upon showing that there is no substantial possibility they could use their monopoly power to impede competition in the additional markets. Authorization to do so is called a line of business waiver.

line-side connection. A connection to a telecommunications switch generally used to connect terminal equipment. Line-side connections are typically two-wire connections.

line turnaround. The reversing of transmission direction from sender to receiver or vice versa when using a half-duplex circuit.

link access procedure balanced (LAPB). A standard link-level protocol that is used to support CCITT X.25 packet-switching.

link access procedure for the D-channel (LAPD). *See* Q.921

LMS. *See* local measured service

loaded line. A telephone line equipped with loading coils to add inductance in order to minimize amplitude distortion.

LOB. *See* line of business waiver

local access and transport area (LATA). Subsequent to Divestiture, the territory served by the various BOCs is divided into approximately 160 exchanges called local access and transport areas (LATAs). The MFJ specifies that the BOCs offer regulated telecommunications services within LATAs, while AT&T and other interexchange carriers offer services between LATAs.

local area data transport (LADT). Use of the local loop to provide both data and analog voice services for subscribers.

local area network (LAN). A system linking together computers, word processors and other electronic office machines and workstations to create an intraoffice, or intrasite network. LANs often provide access to external networks.

local channel. A private-line facility contained within a single LATA and used to interconnect telephone company central offices. These circuits are typically used to connect local-loop facilities terminating in one central office to another central office where access to interexchange carrier facilities can be accommodated. For example, a subscriber location might be connected to the telephone company central office via private-line local-loop facilities, which would be connected to another central office within the same LATA using a private-line local channel, where connection to the interexchange carrier network would be accomplished.

local company. *See* local exchange carrier

local exchange area. *See* exchange area

local exchange carrier (LEC). A carrier providing local exchange service.

local exchange service. Telephone service provided within a local exchange area.

local loop. A telecommunications channel connecting the subscriber's equipment to the line-terminating equipment in the telephone company central office.

local measured service (LMS). A usage-sensitive method of pricing local telephone calls, usually dependent on distance and time.

long-distance service. *See* interexchange service

longitudinal redundancy check (LRC). An error detection scheme in which the check character consists of bits calculated on the basis of odd and even parity on all the characters of the block, dependent upon the protocol in use.

loopback test. A test conducted on a telecommunications channel wherein the receive channel is connected to the transmit channel at the distant end to enable test signals imposed on the channel to be received and analyzed at the same proximate location.

LRC. *See* longitudinal redundancy check

mark. The presence of signal. In telegraph communications, a mark represents the closed condition or current flowing. A mark impulse is equivalent to a binary 1. *See also* space

Mbps. *See* megabits per second

MCC. *See* miscellaneous common carrier

Mead Data Central. Information service [Mead Data Central, 9333 Springboro Pike, P.O. Box 933, Dayton, Ohio 45401].

megabits per second (Mbps). One million bits per second.

megaHertz (MHz). One million Hertz, or one million cycles per second.

Memorandum Opinion & Order (MO&O). Under FCC procedures a Memorandum Opinion & Order is issued with the intent of closing a matter. An MO&O usually takes one of two forms: Memorandum Opinion & Order Denying Petition which, baring a petition for reconsideration, gives notice of rejection of a petition to the Commission, and Memorandum Opinion & Order Concluding Inquiry, which is used to conclude a Notice of Inquiry.

message switch. A telecommunications switching device used to support store and forward messaging techniques.

message telecommunications service (MTS). Nonprivate intrastate and interstate long-distance telephone service.

MFJ. *See* Modified Final Judgment

MHz. *See* megaHertz

microwave. A term loosely applied to those radio frequency wavelengths which are sufficiently short to exhibit some of the properties of light. Commonly used for frequencies from one billion cycles per second, or gigaHertz (GHz), to 30 GHz.

minimum point of penetration (MPOP). *See* minimum point of termination

minimum point of termination (MPOT). The point necessary to bring regulated telecommunications services to the customer or building owner.

miscellaneous common carrier (MCC). A communications common carrier which is not engaged in the business of providing either public land-line message telephone service or public telegraph service.

modem. A contraction of *mod*ulator-*dem*odulator. A telecommunications device that translates digital electrical signals into audio signals for transmission over telephone lines, and the reverse process for incoming signals.

modem eliminator. A device which interfaces between a local terminal that normally requires a modem and the computer near it that also expects to connect to a modem. The device functions as an imitation modem in both directions.

Modified Final Judgment (MFJ). *See* Divestiture

modulator-demodulator (modem). *See* modem

Monopoly service. Telecommunications service provided by a carrier solely authorized by a government regulating body to provide the service within a specified area or jurisdiction.

MO&O. *See* Memorandum Opinion & Order

MPLS. *See* multischedule private line schedule

MPOP. *See* minimum point of penetration

MPOT. *See* minimum point of termination

MTS. *See* message telecommunications service

multidrop line (a.k.a. multipoint line). A single communications line or circuit interconnecting several stations. Use of this type of line usually requires some kind of polling mechanism to address each terminal with a unique address code.

multiplexing. A process for combining a number of individual channels into a common frequency band or into a common bit stream for transmission. *See also* demultiplexing

multiplexor. A device that performs multiplexing.

multipoint line. *See* multidrop line

multischedule private line schedule (MPLS). A rate schedule for AT&T intercity private-line service which replaced the Hi-Lo tariff. MPLS imposes a fixed charge for the first mile of service that is significantly greater than the charge for additional miles. MPLS has since been replaced by AT&T FCC Tariffs Nos. 9, 10, & 11.

NAK. *See* negative acknowledgment

National Exchange Carriers Association (NECA). An organization created by the FCC in March 1983, to oversee the collection, distribution (to local telephone companies) and review of access charges billed to the interexchange carriers and end users.

NECA. *See* National Exchange Carriers Association

negative acknowledgment (NAK). A transmission control character transmitted by a receiver as a negative response to the sender.

network interface (NI). *See* public network demarcation point

network termination 1 (NT1). The customer-premises equipment (CPE) that provides the physical termination of the integrated services digital network (ISDN) transmission line, converts between layer 1 formats used at the U and T reference points, and performs some maintenance functions.

network termination 2 (NT2). The customer-premises equipment (CPE) that performs the functions of a customer-premises switch or multiplexor within an integrated services digital network (ISDN).

new social contract. A regulatory concept in which local basic service rates are fixed, and often other guarantees made by the local carrier, in turn for relaxation or elimination of regulation in other service areas.

NI. *See* network interface

node. A point of interconnection to a network. Normally, a point at which a number of terminals or tail circuits attach to the network.

NOI. *See* Notice of Inquiry

nondominant common carrier. A carrier not having control over a substantial portion, or subportion, of the telecommunications market. A carrier that does not have significant market power. Generally speaking, this includes all carriers other than AT&T and the BOCs in the voice telecommunications market.

nonreturn-to-zero encoding (NRZ). Pulses in alternating directions for successive 1 bits but no change from existing bias for 0 bits.

nonstructural safeguards. A regulatory concept wherein cross-subsidization of services is supposedly prohibited by means of accounting and other administrative procedures in lieu of the requirement for separate operating subsidiary organizations. *See also* structural safeguards

nontraffic sensitive (NTS) costs. Telecommunications network costs that are independent of the amount of traffic carried (i.e., fixed costs).

Notice of Inquiry (NOI). Under FCC procedures, the Commission issues a Notice of Inquiry when it is simply asking for information on a broad subject or trying to generate ideas on a given topic. The NOI is published in the *Federal Register* and a Docket instituted. Adequate time for response by interested parties is then allowed. A NOI must be followed by either a Notice of Proposed Rule Making or a Memorandum Opinion and Order Concluding Inquiry.

Notice of Proposed Rule Making (NPRM; Notice). Title 5 of the United States Code establishes procedures which agencies such as the FCC must follow for rule making (i.e., the process of formulating, amending, or repealing regulations). 5 U.S.C., Sec. 553 requires that general notice of proposed rule making be published in the *Federal Register* as a part of this process. Adequate time for response by interested parties must then be allowed (30 days for substantive rules) before the rule becomes effective under most circumstances. Under FCC procedures, a NPRM is issued and a Docket established when there is a specific change to the rules being proposed. *See also* Notice of Inquiry

NPRM. *See* Notice of Proposed Rule Making

NRZ. *See* nonreturn-to-zero encoding

NT1. *See* network termination 1

NT2. *See* network termination 2

NTS. *See* nontraffic sensitive costs

null modem. *See* modem eliminator

OCC. *See* other common carrier

OCLC. Information service [OCLC Online Computer Library Center, Inc., 6565 Frantz Road, Dublin Ohio 43017, (614) 764-6000].

O-minus call. A long-distance call wherein the caller dials 0 and waits for an operator to come onto the line.

ONA. *See* open network architecture

open network architecture (ONA). As a result of computer inquiry III, the FCC imposed new rules in place of structural safeguards requiring AT&T and the Bell operating companies (BOCs) to offer enhanced services based on a new model, called open network architecture, and further required them to submit ONA plans by February 1, 1988. ONA would eliminate the requirement for AT&T and the BOCs to provide enhances service through separate subsidiaries.

Open System Interconnection (OSI). An internationally agreed model for data systems that interwork which uses a standard set of protocols developed by the International Standards Organization (ISO).

O-plus call. A long-distance call wherein the caller dials 0 plus the long-distance number being called, and waits for an operator to come onto the line to take a credit-card number — or, with some equipment, simply dials the credit card number when a bong tone is heard.

OSI. *See* Open System Interconnection

other common carrier (OCC). A telecommunications common carrier (other than AT&T) authorized by the FCC to provide a variety of telecommunications services. The FCC refers to these carriers as Domestic satellite carriers (DSC), Miscellaneous common carriers (MCC), and Specialized common carriers (SCC).

PABX. *See* private (automated) branch exchange

packet. A group of binary digits, including data and call control signals, which is switched as a whole. The packet information is arranged in a specific format.

packet assembler/disassembler (PAD). A device that accepts character input and assembles packets for transmission on a packet network, and the reverse. PADs often are used on X.25 packet networks to enable asynchronous character-oriented devices to access the X.25 network.

packet switch. A telecommunications switching device used to switch and route data packets within a packet data network.

packet-switched service. *See* packet data network

packet data network (PDN). A switched network which provides connections by forwarding standard data packets between user parties. A packet is a collection of data and control characters in a specified format, which are transferred as a whole. *See also* value-added network

PAD. *See* packet assembler/disassembler

parallel transmission. Byte-wise data transmission that allocates a data line for each bit in a word. Transmission is usually unidirectional.

parity. The sense of the sum of a series of bits — odd or even. If the sum is odd it is said to have odd parity, and visa verse for even parity. Often in telecommunications an additional bit, called a parity bit, is added to a character or block of data which is arbitrarily assigned a value to ensure the parity of the character or block is preserved. Hence if the received data are found to have incorrect parity, an error is determined to have occurred. Typically odd parity is used in synchronous transmission schemes and even in asynchronous schemes.

PBX. *See* private branch exchange

PCM. *See* pulse code modulation

PDN. *See* packet data network

phase. The attribute of a sine wave having to do with its starting point in time.

phase modulation. One of three ways of modifying a sine wave signal to make it carry information. The sine wave or carrier has its phase changed in accordance with the information to be transmitted.

point-to-point. A connection between two, and only two, terminals or computers.

polling. A means of terminal control on a multidrop line by sequential inquiry.

port. An interface on a computer configured as data terminal equipment and capable of attaching a modem for communication with a remote data terminal. Also, to modify a software program so as to function in a different computer environment from that for which it was designed; to transport the program.

postal, telegraph, and telephone authority (PTT). A generic term for the government-operated common carriers in countries other than the United States and Canada.

preemption (a.k.a. federal supremacy). A legal concept that asserts precedence of federal jurisdictional authority over local or state jurisdictional authority when elements of interstate commerce are determined to exist.

premises wiring. *See* inside wire

presubscription. The capability of a subscriber to select to which long-distance carrier traffic will be routed when the subscriber dials 1 plus the long-distance number. The subscriber can specify another carrier by Gypsy calling.

PRI. *See* primary rate interface

price-cap regulation. A regulatory concept wherein restrictions are placed on the aggregate price of a group of telecommunications services, rather than regulating the rate-of-return on the investments of the carrier. *See also* rate-of-return regulation

price parity. A regulatory concept wherein a local exchange carrier would be allowed to provide enhanced services without allowing other enhanced service providers to collocate equipment at the local exchange carrier's central office, provided that the carrier charge itself the same rates it would otherwise charge the enhanced service provider for the same services.

primary rate interface (PRI). The integrated services digital network (ISDN) interface that connects high-capacity CPE, such as PBXs, to the network; within the United States, it is composed of 23 64-Kbps B-channels and one 64-Kbps D-channel. PRI is synonymous with 23B+D.

private branch exchange (PBX). A private switching system, either manual or automatic, usually serving an organization, such as a business or a government agency, and usually located on the customer's premises.

private line. A circuit (or line), not interconnected with the public switched telephone network, for the exclusive use of an individual or organization. A Private line may be used for the transmission of voice, data, television, etc.

private network. A telecommunications network for the exclusive use of an individual or organization.

private system. *See* private network

Pro-America tariff. A tariff proposed by AT&T which would allow a price reduction on long-distance calls to users willing to pay a monthly up front fee.

programmable read-only memory (PROM). Nonvolatile (i.e., not alterable) memory, typically a memory chip, that allows a program to be entered once and henceforth to reside permanently in a piece of hardware.

PROM. *See* programmable read-only memory

protocol. A formal set of conventions governing the formatting and relative timing of message exchange between two communicating systems.

PTT. *See* postal, telegraph, and telephone authority

public dial telephone network. A network shared among many users, any of whom can establish communications between desired points, when required, by use of a dial or push-button telephone.

public network demarcation point. The point of connection of telecommunications wiring contained within a building or complex to the public network. Also, the point where the LEC's regulated responsibility ends and nonregulated customer responsibility begins.

pulse code modulation (PCM). Transmission of information by modulation of a pulsed, or intermittent carrier. Pulse width, count, phase, or amplitude may be the varied characteristic. Also, a common form of speech digitization, wherein the analog voice signal is sampled 8,000 times per second and encoded into 8 bits of digital information resulting in the transmission of a 64 Kbps bit stream.

Q.921. A CCITT/OSI layer 2 protocol used on the integrated services digital network (ISDN) D-channel. Q.921 is synonymous with LAPD.

Q.931. A CCITT/OSI layer 3 protocol used on the integrated services digital network (ISDN) D-channel for signaling.

queue. A waiting line or area. Also, to place information into such a waiting line or area.

R reference point. Non-ISDN DTE connects to an integrated services digital network (ISDN) at the R reference point through a terminal adapter *See also* TE2

RAM. *See* random access memory

random access memory (RAM). Read-write dynamically addressable storage. Usually a semiconductor volatile memory wherein data are lost if power is turned off.

rate base. Generally speaking, the current sum of capital investment by a carrier in plant and other facilities necessary to provide a regulated service. Under rate-of-return regulation, it is the rate base upon which the allowed rate of return is applied to determine the allowed earnings of the telephone company for that service.

rate-of-return regulation. A regulatory concept wherein restrictions are placed on the profits of a regulated carrier that are based on the amount of investment made by the carrier. Under this scheme, operating costs of the carrier fall directly into the regulated rate paid by subscribers.

RBOC. *See* regional Bell holding company

RCC. *See* regulated common carrier

read only (RO). A teleprinter receiver with no transmission capability.

read-only memory (ROM). Nonvolatile (e.g., nonalterable) storage, usually semiconductor chip memory, manufactured with a predetermined data content permanently stored.

receive line signal detector. A modem interface signal defined in the EIA RS-232-C standard which indicates to the attached data terminal equipment that it is receiving a signal from the distant modem.

redundancy check. A technique of error detection involving the transmission of additional data related to the basic data in such a way that the receiving terminal, by comparing the two sets of data, can determine to a certain degree of probability whether an error has occurred in transmission. *See also* cyclic redundancy check; vertical redundancy check; longitudinal redundancy check

regeneration. The term applied to the reconstruction and amplification of digital signals. Regeneration differs from simple amplification in that the digital nature of the signal allows for amplification of the signal alone, without any significant accompanying noise.

regional Bell holding company (RBOC; RHC). The MFJ or Divestiture agreement does not prohibit the consolidation of ownership of the BOCs into any particular number of entities. After study by a committee of AT&T and BOC officers, the structure adopted organizes the 22 post-Divestiture BOCs into seven regional holding companies (RHCs) or regional Bell operating companies (RBOCs). The RBOCs operate as holding companies that hold the stock of the BOCs in their respective regions.

regulated common carrier (RCC). A common carrier that is subject to government regulation. AT&T Communications and the BOCs are RCCs.

regulatory flexibility. A regulatory concept wherein the regulatory body, the carrier, or both are allowed certain flexibility in establishing rates, terms, and conditions for regulated services offered.

request to send (RTS). A physical modem interface control signal from the DTE, requesting clearance to transmit.

resale/shared use order. A 1976 FCC decision which declared unlawful virtually all restrictions on the resale and shared use of common carrier interstate private-line services. Resale carriers were subsequently allowed to order services from established telephone common carriers and resell these services to individual users for a profit. The order also permitted shared use, a nonprofit arrangement whereby several users collectively subscribed to private-line services of an established telephone common carrier, with each paying a share of the communications related costs associated with these services.

response time. The elapsed time between the generation of the last character of a message at a terminal and the receipt of the first character of the reply. It includes terminal delay and network delay.

revenue requirement. Under rate-of-return regulation, investment in plant and other facilities, operating costs, and the allowed earnings of the telephone company, that would result from provision of forecasted volumes of offered services, are combined to determine the regulated revenue requirement. This is then divided by the forecasted volume to determine the regulated per-unit rate for the services.

reverse interrupt (RVI). A transmission control character transmitted by a receiving station to request termination of the current transmission because of another high priority message it must send.

RHC. *See* regional Bell holding company

ring indicator (RI). A modem interface signal defined in the EIA RS-232-C standard which indicates to the attached data terminal equipment that an incoming call is present.

riser cable. Telecommunications wiring used to connect different floors in the same building.

RLIN. Information service [Research Library Information Network, the Research Libraries Group (RLG), Jordan Quadrangle, Stanford, California 94305, (415) 328-0920].

RO. *See* read only

ROM. *See* read-only memory

RS-232. The (EIA) industry standard for a 25-pin interface that connects computers and various forms of peripheral equipment, for example modems, printers, etc. Several revisions (e.g., RS-232-C) of the standard have been effected.

RS-449. The (EIA) industry standard for a 37-pin interface that connects computers and various forms of peripheral equipment, for example modems, printers, etc. It is designed for higher speed transmission than the RS-232 interface. Each signal pin has its own return line, instead of a common ground return and the signal pairs (i.e., signal, return) are balanced lines rather than a signal referenced to ground. The associated cable typically uses twisted-pair wire, which a RS-232 cable typically does not use.

RTS. *See* request to send

RVI. *See* reverse interrupt

S reference point. Integrated service digital network (ISDN) terminals may connect to the network at the S or T reference points associated with an NT1 or NT2. The S and T reference points use identical protocols and, in the case where an NT2 is not used, refer to the same physical point. *See* also TE1

SCC. *See* specialized common carrier

SDLC. *See* synchronous data link control

SDN. *See* software-defined network

Section 214. A section of the Communications Act of 1934 dealing with the construction or acquisition of lines. Section 214 requires carriers to obtain a certificate (214 Certificate of Authority) from the FCC, prior to construction or extension of lines, or acquisition or operation of lines, stating that such undertakings are required to satisfy the present or future public convenience and necessity.

separations procedures. Allocation of costs by various regulatory agencies between state and federal jurisdictions.

serial transmission. A method of data transmission in which each bit of information is sent sequentially on a single data channel. Serial transmission is the normal transmission mode for data communications.

service interface (SI). The point where the LEC's service responsibility ends. The SI differs from the network interface, in that the facilities between the NI and the SI may not be owned by the LEC.

shared tenant services (STS). Telephone services for building or office park tenants provided from a facility within the same building or complex. An in-house telephone company (or service co.) for office buildings, industrial complexes, or shopping malls.

shared use. *See* resale/shared use order

shift-in character (SI). A control character used in conjunction with SO and ESC characters to extend the graphic character set.

shift-out character (SO). A control character used in conjunction with SI and ESC to extend the graphic character set.

simplex circuit. A telecommunications circuit that conducts signals in only one direction.

short-haul modem. A signal converter which conditions a digital signal to ensure reliable transmission over DC continuous private line metallic circuits without interfering with adjacent pairs in the same telephone cable.

SI. *See* shift-in character

Signaling System No. 7 (SS#7). A new international standard (CCITT Q.700 series) common channel (out-of-band) signaling, or CCS, being developed in parallel with ISDN to support signaling between network switches. Out-of-band call signaling between the customer equipment and the ISDN network are supported by a modified form of CCITT X.25's LAPB (CCITT Q.921, or LAPD) link-level protocol, and a new protocol for the network services layer (CCITT Q.931).

signal transfer point (STP). A node on a tandem network where trunks from an access switch are connected to the tandem network. For example, trunks from one or more PBXs, packet switches, etc. might be connected to a tandem network at the STP.

simple wire. Telephone wiring installed in residences or single-line businesses.

sine wave. The simplest type of wave. An analog waveform that can be represented mathematically by a sine function. An analog waveform used to represent simple harmonic motion as a function of time, or the two-dimensional projection of uniform circular motion as a function of time.

smart modem. Generally speaking, a modem that has integral processing capability. Smart modems are generally capable of accepting and executing commands (e.g., dialing a number, answering a call, setting or changing speed or other parameters, etc.), and often can perform other more sophisticated functions such as buffering and storage of data as well as frequently called numbers, error detection and/or correction, data compression and decompression, etc.

SO. *See* shift-out character

software-defined network (SDN). AT&T facility by which major customers can use part of the AT&T Communications network for their own dedicated internal voice and data systems. SDN allows many of the advantages of a private network while using the public network.

SOH. *See* start-of-header character

space. The absence of signal. In telegraph communications, a space represents the open condition or no current flowing. A space impulse is equivalent to a binary 0. *See also* mark

space segment. That portion of a satellite-based telecommunications link between the earthstation and the satellite, not including the earthstation, or other terrestrial links and equipment.

SPC. *See* stored program control

special access. Facilities, other than the local switched telephone network, used to provide access to public or private interexchange network facilities.

special access surcharge. A surcharge, currently $25 per month per end, imposed on special access facilities that can leak traffic onto the local switched network *See also* leaky PBX

specialized common carrier (SCC). An intercity communications common carrier, other than an established telephone common carrier, authorized by the FCC to provide private-line communications services in competition with established telephone common carriers.

spectrum. The range or series of frequencies characterized by electromagnetic radiation. Also a given range of frequencies of electromagnetic radiation sharing a common characteristic (e.g., light spectrum, microwave spectrum, radio spectrum, etc.), or defined by custom or regulation (e.g., FM radio spectrum).

splashed call. An call, usually long-distance, that is originally intercepted by an alternative operator service, back-hauled to the operations center of the AOS, where it is determined that the caller requires that the call be carried by another carrier. The call is then transferred to the requested carrier, but at the location of the AOS's switch which usually is in a location different from the originating call due to the previous back-hauling. Such a splashed call is subsequently billed by the latter carrier as having originated at the point the call was transferred to that carrier, and not at the location that the caller placed the call on the AOS network.

SS#7. *See* Signaling System No. 7

start bit. A longer-than-normal bit used in asynchronous communications to signal the beginning of a transmission. It is used in conjunction with the stop bit to define a series of data bits.

start-of-header character (SOH). A transmission control character which is used as the first character of a heading of an information message.

start-of-text character (STX). A transmission control character, which precedes a text, used to terminate a heading.

statistical multiplexing. A multiplexing technique which takes advantage of the statistical nature of arrivals of data elements on two or more channels to achieve improved common channel utilization.

stop bit. A longer-than-normal bit used in asynchronous communications to signal the end of a series of data bits. Together, the start bit and stop bit define a unit of information being transmitted.

stored program control (SPC). A form of switching system control in which system operations are controlled by a stored program executed by one or more processors. Operation of the system can be altered significantly by changing programs.

store and forward. A messaging technique wherein messages are received and stored, generally in electronic form, to be delivered to the intended recipient at some later time.

strategic pricing. The flexibility given to regulated carriers to pick and choose how they will recover subsidies to meet the cost/price differential imposed by agreed to price conditions on certain specific services.

STS. *See* shared tenant services

structural separations. The requirement that certain products or services be provided by separate subsidiaries. *See also* structural safeguards

structural safeguards. The regulatory concept that protection from nonallowed cross-subsidization of telecommunications services or products can be achieved by requiring the separate services or products to be provided by separate subsidiaries. *See also* nonstructural safeguards

STX. *See* start-of-text character

switched access. Access to interexchange networks via the local switched telephone network.

SYN. *See* synchronous idle character

synchronous data link control (SDLC). The IBM standard communications protocol superseding BSC.

synchronous idle character (SYN). A transmission control character used by a synchronous transmission system in the absence of any other character (idle condition) to provide a signal. SYN may also be used by synchronous transmission systems to establish synchronization between transmitter and receiver.

synchronous transmission. Transmission in which the data characters and bits are transmitted at a fixed rate with the transmitter and receiver synchronized. *See also* asynchronous transmission

T reference point. Integrated service digital network (ISDN) terminals may connect to the network at the S or T reference points associated with an NT1 or NT2. The S and T reference points use identical protocols and, in the case where an NT2 is not used, refer to the same physical point. *See also* TE1

TA. *See* terminal adapter

tail circuit. A feeder circuit or an access line to a network node.

tandem network. A network that connects and switches trunk circuits. Generally speaking, a tandem network connects to other access switches (e.g., PBXs) and provides and switches trunk circuits between these access switches.

tandem switch. A switch in a tandem network. A switch that provides only trunk connections (i.e., does not make provision for line-side connections).

tariff. The applicable published rates, regulations, and descriptions governing the provision of regulated and tariffed communications service. However, not all regulated communications service is provided subject to tariff.

T-carrier. A series of transmission systems using pulse code modulation technology at various channel capacities and bit rates (e.g., T-1, T-2, T-3, or T-4). T-carrier channels are high capacity digital channels ranging from 1.544 Mbps for T-1 to 274.176 Mbps for T-4, or 24 to 4,032 equivalent voice channels respectively. The term is often used with regard to specific AT&T transmission formats.

TE1. *See* terminal equipment type 1

TE2. *See* terminal equipment type 2

terminal adapter (TA). A customer-premises equipment (CPE) device that links integrated services digital network (ISDN) services with non-ISDN DTE.

terminal equipment type 1 (TE1). Integrated services digital network (ISDN) compatible terminal equipment.

terminal equipment type 2 (TE2). Terminal equipment that is not compatible with an integrated services digital network (ISDN) that is connected at EIA RS-232, RS-449, or CCITT V.35 interfaces.

termination charge. *See* access charge

TDM. *See* time-division multiplexing

telephone closet. A room, or other facility, used to house the equipment necessary to connect wires leading to terminal equipment locations with the public telephone network, or with larger facilities leading to the network or other telephone closets.

teleport. A project, often developed by a municipal authority, which provides a metropolitan area with satellite communications.

teletype exchange (telex). An automatic teletype-exchange service where subscribers can dial each other for direct, two-way telemeter communications.

telex. *See* teletype exchange

Telpak tariff. An AT&T tariff that provided substantial discounts (51%, 64%, 77%, and 85% respectively) for the lease of 12 (Telpak A), 24 (Telpak B), 60 (Telpak C), or 240 (Telpak D) telecommunications channels within one facility. The FCC found Telpak A and B to be unjustified and cancelled them in 1964. In 1976, the FCC found Telpak C and D to be illegal and ordered them withdrawn by June 1977.

terminal. Equipment at the end of a telecommunications circuit (i.e., upon which the circuit is terminated), including telephone sets and computer terminals.

terminal equipment. *See* data terminal equipment

thermal noise. Random electrical signals or noise related to the operating temperature of electrical circuit elements. The basis for this phenomenon is the random motion of charged particles (e.g., electrons) in the circuit elements themselves due to temperature.

tie line (a.k.a. tie trunk). *See* interlocation trunking

time-division multiplexing (TDM). A technique for sharing a telecommunications channel wherein only one station at a time is allowed to use the channel for transmission of information, but where two or more stations are allowed to transmit information at different points in time. *See also* frequency-division multiplexing

token passing. A time-division multiplexing technique often used in local area networks based on the principle that to use the network, a station must possess a single electronic token. The token is passed in a systematic way between the stations on the network, so only one station at a time is allowed to transmit data.

touch-tone. *See* dual-tone multifrequency

traffic sensitive costs. Telecommunications network costs that depend upon the volume of traffic carried.

transient. *See* electrical transient

transceiver. An abbreviation for transmitter/receiver. A device that functions both as a telecommunications transmitter and receiver.

trunk. The telecommunications circuit between two network nodes or switches (e.g., between telephone company central offices).

trunk-side connection. A connection to a telecommunications switch typically used to connect the switch to another switching device or network. Trunk-side connections are typically four-wire connections.

turnaround time. The actual time required to reverse the direction of transmission from sender to receiver or vice versa when using a half-duplex circuit. Time is required for line propagation effects, modem timing, and computer reaction.

twisted pair wire. A pair of wires used in transmission circuits and twisted about one another to minimize coupling with other circuits.

two-wire connection. A telecommunications circuit that consists of two-physical wires — usually a twisted-pair wire. Generally signals flow both ways in the loop simultaneously (*See* full-duplex circuit), although sometimes signals flow only one way (*See* simplex circuit), or alternately in one direction at a time (*See* half-duplex circuit)

U reference point. The point of connection of customer-premises equipment (CPE) to the exchange termination and transmission line in an integrated services digital network (ISDN). Under United States regulations, the U reference point marks the line of demarcation between customer-owned equipment and the public network.

ultra small aperture terminal (USAT). Small receive-only or transmit-receive satellite earthstations, usually less than one meter in diameter, and normally used in private telecommunications networks. Typically, many USATs separately communicate with a single large diameter hub earthstation using a satellite link, with switching and other control and management functions being performed at the hub location.

unbundled services. Products or services offered in their smallest useful configuration. Telecommunications products or services offered in such a manner as to make it possible to choose between competitive offerings and interconnect the resulting services in a useful manner.

USAT. *See* ultra small aperture terminal

V.110. A CCITT data-transfer protocol for the B-channel within an integrated services digital network (ISDN).

V.120. A CCITT data-transfer protocol for the B-channel within an integrated services digital network (ISDN).

V.35. A CCITT standard specification for data transmission at 48 Kbps.

value-added network (VAN). A data communications system in which services provided for users greatly enhance the usefulness of the basic facilities utilized.

value-based pricing. Pricing of products or services based upon their perceived value. The pricing of various regulated telecommunications services based upon aggregate costs, but with the prices for specific services reflecting perceived value and not necessarily directly related to the cost to provide the specific service. For example, the pricing of basic telephone service below the cost to provide that service and subsidizing the service with long-distance service.

VAN. *See* value-added network.

vertical redundancy check (VRC). An error detection scheme in which the parity bit of each character is set to 1 or 0 so that the total number of 1 bits in the character is odd or even as determined by the protocol in use.

vertical tabulation character (VT). A format effector which advances the active position to the same character position on the next predetermined line.

very small aperture terminal (VSAT). Small receive-only or transmit-receive satellite earthstations, usually less than two meters in diameter, and normally used in private telecommunications networks. Typically, many VSATs separately communicate with a single large diameter hub earthstation using a satellite link, with switching and other control and management functions being performed at the hub location.

videotex. An interactive information retrieval system where data are transmitted over telephone wires between a distant computer and home television units.

virtual private network (VPN). A private network that utilizes the public network facilities in such a way as to appear to use dedicated private facilities. This technology offers many of the benefits of a private network while also taking advantage of benefits offered by the switched public network. *See also* software-defined network

voice mail. The capability to store and retrieve voice messages using a telephone system. A typical system provides a user with a voice mailbox, where callers can leave voice messages to be retrieved at some later time by the user.

VPN. *See* virtual private network

VRC. *See* vertical redundancy check

VSAT. *See* very small aperture terminal

VT. *See* vertical tabulation character

WATS. *See* wide area telecommunications service

waveguide. A metal tube utilized for transmission of very high frequency electromagnetic signals.

white noise. Random electrical (or sometimes acoustical) signals or noise.

wide area telecommunications service (WATS). A service that permits customers to make (OUTWATS) or receive (INWATS or 800 service) long-distance calls and to have them billed on a bulk basis rather than individually.

word. A data element consisting of a defined number of bits. A word typically consists of 8 bits or 1 byte, 16 bits or 2 bytes, 32 bits or 4 bytes, or 64 bits or 8 bytes.

X.PC. A network interface specification, described by Tymnet, that specifies a protocol for accessing an X.25 network using a switched access line. *See also* X.25; X.32

X.3. The CCITT standard that describes Packet Assembler/Disassembler (PAD) parameters.

X.25. The CCITT standard interface protocol for packet data networks that defines the message structure required by data terminal equipment (DTE) to interface to a public packet network conforming to CCITT standards. The X.25 standard consists of three levels of protocol: the physical layer, the link layer, and the network (or packet) layer. These three levels conform to the lower three layers of the International Standards Organization (ISO) seven-layer reference model for open system interconnection (OSI).

X.28. The CCITT standard that describes the data terminal equipment (DTE)-to-packet assembler/disassembler (PAD) protocol.

X.29. The CCITT standard that describes the host packet assembler (PAD)-to-terminal PAD protocol.

X.31. The CCITT standard interface that describes how packet data terminal equipment (DTE) connect to an integrated services digital network (ISDN).

X.32. The CCITT standard that describes how X.25 packet data terminal equipment (DTE) access an X.25 packet data network using a switched access line.

X.75. The CCITT standard interface protocol for packet data networks that defines the message structure required for gateway nodes of public packet networks to intercommunicate.

X.121. An international standard for numbering networks and stations that will be interconnected using the X.25 and related protocols.

Xoff character. The communication control character used to instruct a terminal to suspend transmission.

Xon character. The communications control character used to instruct a terminal to start or resume transmission.

Bibliography

"A History of the Telecommunications Regulatory Environment." In *Datapro Management of Telecommunications*. Delran, New Jersey: Datapro Research Corporation, Report No. MT10-620-101 (1987):101.

American Library Association. "Comments of the American Library Association." *Filing and Review of Open Network Architecture Plans,* Federal Communications Commission, CC Docket No. 88-2, Phase I and II. Washington, D.C. (1988).

Angel, Albert J. "Competition Intensifies in Operator Services." *Business Communications Review.* Hinsdale, Illinois: BCR Enterprises 18(2) (1988):52.

"An Overview of Interstate Long Distance Facilities." In *Datapro Management of Telecommunications*. Delran, New Jersey: Datapro Research Corporation, Report No. MT20-500-101 (1986):101.

"AOS Services Attract Attention." In *Datapro Management of Telecommunications*. Delran, New Jersey: Datapro Research Corporation, Report No. MT99-801-062 (1988):1.

"At Least Five States Planning Summer Hearings on Regulation of AOS Business." *State Telephone Regulation Report.* Alexandria, Virginia: Capitol Publications, Inc. 6(13) (1988):5.

"AT&T Announces Products Targeted to Growing Markets for Central Office LAN Services." *Telecommunications Reports.* New York: Business Research Publications, Inc. 54(47) (1988):20.

"AT&T Files '800 Information Forwarding-1' Service for Pay-Per-View Cable Industry." *Telecommunications Reports.* New York: Business Research Publications, Inc. 54(18) (1988):24.

"AT&T Gearing Up to Offer Capabilities for MEGACOM, MEGACOM '800,' ACCUNET Switched Digital Service; Tariff Filing Outlines 'Primary Rate Interface,' Two Optional Features." *Telecommunications Reports.* New York: Business Research Publications, Inc. 54(14) (1988):7.

"AT&T, NATA Oppose Requests for Reconsideration of Inside Wire Detariffing, Preemption." *Telecommunications Reports*. New York: Business Research Publications, Inc. 53(8) (1987):20.

"AT&T 'ONA' Plan Outlines Compliance with 'CEI' Requirements, Network Capability for InterLATA Transport of 'Basic Service Elements'; Current Technical Limitations Cited." *Telecommunications Reports*. New York: Business Research Publications, Inc. 54(5) (1988):16.

"AT&T Says Privacy Concerns Should Not Be a Factor in FCC Review of INFO-2 Service." *Telecommunications Reports*. New York: Business Research Publications, Inc. 54(22) (1988):25.

Bartlett, John. *Familiar Quotations,* 15th. Edition. Boston: Little, Brown & Company, 1980.

Bass, Charlie and Berkowitz, Paul. "What Does ISDN Compatibility Really Mean?" *TPT Networking Management*. Tulsa: PennWell Publishing Co. 6(12) (1988):32.

Baumol, William J. and Blackman, Sue Anne Batey. "Electronics, the Cost Disease, and the Operation of Libraries." *Journal of the American Society for Information Science*. New York, New York: John Wiley & Sons, Inc. 34(3) (1983):184.

Bernard, Keith E. "Regulatory Development in the U.S." *Journal of the American Society for Information Science*. New York, New York: John Wiley & Sons, Inc. 37(6) (1986):409.

Black Box Catalog. Pittsburgh: Black Box Corp., 1985.

Blundell, Greggory S. "Getting to the Heart of the Bypass Matter." *Data Communications* (extra). New York: McGraw-Hill (1984) 13(12):78.

"BOCs Outline 'Open Network Architecture' Plans in Feb. 1 Filings at FCC; Most Plans Generally Follow BOC/Bellcore Model with Some Differences on Tariff, Pricing Issues." *Telecommunications Reports*. New York: Business Research Publications, Inc. 54(5) (1988):12.

Boss, Richard W. *Telecommunications for Library Management*. White Plains, New York: Knowledge Industry Publications, Inc., 1985.

Bowman, Rex. "ACUTA Members Caution Peers Against AOS Firms." *Network World*. Framingham, Massachusetts: CW Publishing, Inc. 5(30) (1988):4.

Bridge, Robert F. and Stern, Ken. "Getting the Most from Existing Twisted-Pair Transmission Media." *Telecommunications*. Norwood, Massachusetts: Horizon House-Microwave 20(12) (1986):45.

Brock, Gerald W. *The Telecommunications Industry: The Dynamics of Market Structure*. Cambridge: Harvard University Press, 1981.

Brown, Bob. "Users Face Risk from PVC Wire." *Network World*. Framingham, Massachusetts: CW Publishing, Inc. 5(30) (1988):1.

Brown, Rowland C.W. "The Urban Electronic Library in the Emerging Communications Era: Implications for National Networks." In: Ladenson, Alex, ed. *The Urban Electronic Library in the Communications Era*. Chicago: Urban Libraries Council (1984):57.

Brownrigg, Edwin B. [and others]. "Packet Radio for Library Automation." *Information Technology and Libraries*. Chicago: Library and Information Technology Association, American Library Association 3(3) (1984):229.

Brummitt Duggan, Susanne. "SMDR Can Be a Telco's Ace in the Hole." *Telephony*. Chicago: Intertec Publishing 215(1) (1988):26.

Bulnes, Juan. "Local Area Networks." In *Telecommunications for Management*. Meadow, Charles T. and Tedesco, Albert S., eds. New York: McGraw-Hill (1985):143.

"Bypass Technologies." In *Datapro Management of Telecommunications*. Delran, New Jersey: Datapro Research Corporation, Report No. MT20-520-101 (1985):101.

Cacciamani, Eugene R. and Sun, Michael K. "Overview of VSAT Networks." *Telecommunications*. Norwood, Massachusetts: Horizon House-Microwave 20(6) (1986):38.

Camp, Lee G. "Customers' Needs Are Driving the Development of New Technology." *Telecommunications*. Norwood, Massachusetts: Horizon House-Microwave 21(8) (1987):79.

"Central Office Local Area Networks." *This Month in Telecommunications*. Delran, New Jersey: Datapro Research Corporation (1988):7.

"Commission Proposed Part 68 Rule Changes on Customer Installation of Inside Wiring." *Telecommunications Reports*. New York: Business Research Publications, Inc. 54(5) (1988):38.

"Comparing Centrex Service and PBXs." In *Datapro Management of Telecommunications*. Delran, New Jersey: Datapro Research Corporation, Report No. MT40-240-101 (1987):101.

"Comparing PABXs and LANs." In *Datapro Management of Telecommunications*. Delran, New Jersey: Datapro Research Corporation, Report No. MT40-220-101 (1987):101.

Cooley, K.D. [and others]. "Wideband Virtual Networks." *Telecommunications*. Norwood, Massachusetts: Horizon House-Microwave 21(2) (1987):65.

"Critical of Other Providers, Ramada Agrees to Offer Guests AT&T Operator Services." *Telecommunications Reports*. New York: Business Research Publications, Inc. 54(36) (1988):20.

Datapro Research Corp. "Users Rate Their LANs." *Data Communications*. New York: McGraw-Hill 16(6) (1987):106.

DeLong, Edgar S. Jr. "Making 911 Even Better." *Telephony*. Chicago: Intertec Publishing 213(24) (1987):60.

Denenberg, Ray. "Linked Systems Project, Part 2: Standard Network Interconnection." *Library Hi Tech*. Ann Arbor, Michigan: Pierian Press 3(2)10 (1985):71.

Denenberg, Ray. "Open Systems Interconnection." *Library Hi Tech*. Ann Arbor, Michigan: Pierian Press 3(1)9 (1985):15.

Dictionary of Computing, 2nd Edition. New York: Oxford University Press, 1986.

Dooley, Jerry. "The Economics of ISDN." *Network World*. Framingham, Massachusetts: CW Publishing, Inc. 4(33) (1987):9.

Drucker, Peter F. *Management: Tasks, Responsibilities, Practices*. New York: Harper & Row, 1974.

Easton, Anthony T. "The Cellular Telephone Revolution: The Future of Personal Communication." *Telecommunications*. Norwood, Massachusetts: Horizon House-Microwave 21(8) (1987):80.

Edrington, Thomas C., IV. "Project Victoria: Adaptable Technology for Widespread Application." *Telecommunications*. Norwood, Massachusetts: Horizon House-Microwave 20(4) (1986):88.

Ergas, Henry. "Information Technology Standards: The Issues." *Telecommunications*. Norwood, Massachusetts: Horizon House-Microwave 20(9) (1986):127.

Estrin, Judith. "The Future of Local Area Networks." *Telecommunications*. Norwood, Massachusetts: Horizon House-Microwave 21(8) (1987):68.

"Evolution of the Public Switched Telephone Network: From Analog to Digital." In *Datapro Management of Telecommunications*. Delran, New Jersey: Datapro Research Corporation, Report No. MT20-305-101 (1985):101.

"FCC Affirms Inside Wire Detariffing, State Preemption; Ends Mandatory Relinquishment." *Telecommunications Reports*. New York: Business Research Publications, Inc. 52(47) (1986):19.

"FCC Again Rules Interstate Service Has Precedence in Joint Jurisdictional Offering." *Telecommunications Reports*. New York: Business Research Publications, Inc. 51(33) (1985):11.

"FCC Denies CPUC Motion for Stay of Preemptive Effect of Inside Wire Detariffing Order." *Telecommunications Reports*. New York: Business Research Publications, Inc. 53(1) (1987):11.

"FCC Detariffs Simple Inside Wire, Calls for Nationwide Competition in Maintenance." *Telecommunications Reports*. New York: Business Research Publications, Inc. 52(5) (1986):10.

"FCC Proposes Easing Rules for Customer Inside Wire, Sees Little Risk of Network Harm." *Telecommunications Reports*. New York: Business Research Publications, Inc. 54(10) (1988):22.

"FCC Upholds Preemption of State Regulation of Inside Wiring Installation, Maintenance." *Telecommunications Reports*. New York: Business Research Publications, Inc. 54(11) (1988):24.

Feuer, Sam. "Telecommunications Options for the 1980s." In *Telecommunications Networks: Issues and Trends*. Jacob, M.E.L., ed. White Plains, New York: Knowledge Industry Publications, Inc. (1986):159.

Finneran, Michael F. "A Word About the Wild and Woolly World of Wiring." Data Comm Focus. *Business Communications Review*. Hinsdale, Illinois: BCR Enterprises 17(3) (1987):46.

Finneran, Michael F. "The Central Office: No Man's LAN?" Data Comm Focus. *Business Communications Review*. Hinsdale, Illinois: BCR Enterprises 18(6) (1988):78.

"Fire Resistant Standards Set for Telecom Cable." Industry News. *Communications News*. Cleveland: Edgell Communications 25(9) (1988):19.

Foltz, Harold C.; desJardins, Richard, eds. "The Special Issue on Open Systems Interconnection (OSI) — New International Standards Architecture and Protocols for Distributed Information Systems." *Proceedings of the IEEE*. 71(12) (1983):1331.

Frank, Ronald, ed. *Corporate Strategies for Telecommunications, 1984 & Beyond*. Framingham, Massachusetts: CW Communications, Inc., 1984.

Fredricsson, Staffan. "Fiber-Optic System for Premises Wiring Applications." *Telecommunications*. Norwood, Massachusetts: Horizon House-Microwave 20(12) (1986):39.

Freeman, Roger L. *Telecommunication System Engineering: Analog and Digital Network Design*. New York: John Wiley & Sons, 1980.

Freeman, Roger L. *Telecommunications Transmission Handbook*. 2d ed. New York: John Wiley & Sons, 1981.

Gagliardi, Robert M. *Introduction to Communications Engineering*. New York: John Wiley & Sons, 1978.

Gilhooly, Denis. "The Evolving Packet Network." *Telecommunications*. Norwood, Massachusetts: Horizon House-Microwave 20(12) (1986):52.

Gorman, Michael. "The Organization of Academic Libraries in the Light of Automation." In: Hewitt, Joe A., ed. *Advances in Library Automation and Networking*. Greenwich, Connecticut: JAI Press 1 (1987):151.

Government Organization and Employees. Stat. 378: 429 (Ch. 5).

Griebenow, Allan. "VSAT Implementation from the Buyer's Perspective." *Telecommunications*. Norwood, Massachusetts: Horizon House-Microwave 21(6) (1987):41.

Hammons, D. M. "Where's NECA Going?" *Telephony*. Chicago: Intertec Publishing 207(7) (1984):38.

Hegebarth, Kevin G. "ANI Is the Key to Unlock Advanced Network Services." *Telephony*. Chicago: Intertec Publishing 214(19) (1988):64.

Herman, James G. "Network Management: Old and New." *Telecommunications*. Norwood, Massachusetts: Horizon House-Microwave 21(8) (1987):57.

Herman, James G. [and others]. "Wide Area Networks." *Telecommunications*. Norwood, Massachusetts: Horizon House-Microwave 20(9) (1986):103.

"Intec's Barret Says Staggering Losses from Satellites in Last 20 Months Have Reduced Available Insurance Capacity to Less than Half 1984 Levels, Pushes for Risk Realignment." *Telecommunications Reports*. New York: Business Research Publications, Inc. 51(43) (1985):23.

Johnston, William B. "The Coming Glut of Phone Lines." *Fortune*. New York: Time Inc. 111(1) (1985):96.

Keasler, W.E. [et. al.]. "High Speed Full Duplex Data Transmission Over the Public Switched Telephone Network." *Interface '84 Proceedings: Twelfth Annual Conference & Exposition*; 1984 March 12–15; Las Vegas. New York: McGraw-Hill (1984):44.

Kent, Allen. Resource sharing in libraries. In: Kent, Allen [et. al.], ed. *Encyclopedia of Library and Information Science*. New York: Marcel Dekker 25 (1978):293.

Killette, Kathleen. "Consumers Rally At FCC." *Communications Week*. Manhasset, New York: CMP Publications, Inc. 207 (1988):29.

Killette, Kathleen. "Converging Forces to Change AOS Marketplace, Study Says." Network Services. *Communications Week*. Manhasset, New York: CMP Publications, Inc. 200 (1988):44.

Killette, Kathleen. "FCC Prudent in AOS Probe." *Communications Week*. Manhasset, New York: CMP Publications, Inc. 196 (1988):87.

Killette, Kathleen. "FCC Takes Up Alternative Operator Services." *Communications Week*. Manhasset, New York: CMP Publications, Inc. 191 (1988):54.

Killette, Kathleen. "FCC: OS Action To Be Informal." *Communications Week*. Manhasset, New York: CMP Publications, Inc. 204 (1988):21.

Killette, Kathleen. "Prize with a Price: AT&T Wins HNS Approval." Network Services. *Communications Week*. Manhasset, New York: CMP Publications, Inc. 204 (1988):21.

Knight, Fred S. "The Dark Side of Calling Line ID." *Business Communications Review*. Hinsdale, Illinois: BCR Enterprises 18(5) (1988):6.

Kuehn, Richard A. "Thorny Problems with Calling Cards and Pay Phones." Consultant's Corner. *Business Communications Review*. Hinsdale, Illinois: BCR Enterprises 18(3) (1988):95.

Landauer, Steve. "Data-Over-Voice Multiplexing." *Telecommunications*. Norwood, Massachusetts: Horizon House-Microwave 21(4) (1987):82.

Langley, Graham, ed. *Telephony's Dictionary*. 2d ed. Chicago: Telephony Publishing Corp., 1986.

Learn, Larry L. "Networks: Their Technology, Architecture and Implementation." *Library Hi Tech*. Ann Arbor, Michigan: Pierian Press, 6(2)22 (1988):19–49.

Learn, Larry L. "Networks: The Telecommunications Infrastructure and Impacts of Change." *Library Hi Tech*. Ann Arbor, Michigan: Pierian Press 6(1)21 (1988):13–31.

Learn, Larry L. "The Impact of Advances in Telecommunications on Library and Information Systems." In *Advances in Library Automation and Networking*. Hewitt, Joe A., ed. Greenwich, Connecticut: JAI Press, Inc. 1 (1987):21.

Learn, Larry L. and Lunin, Lois F., eds. "Perspectives On... Telecommunications: Principles, Developments, Prospects." In *Journal of the American Society for Information Science*. New York, New York: John Wiley & Sons, Inc. 37(6) (1986):401.

Learn, Larry L. and McGill, Michael J. "The Telecommunications Environment and Its Implications for System Design." *Microcomputers for Information Management*. Norwood, New Jersey: Ablex Publishing Corporation 1(2) (1984):125.

Lefkon, Dick. "A LAN Primer." *BYTE*. New York: McGraw-Hill 12(8) (1987):147.

Levin, David P. "Creating an Integrated Voice and Data Communications Environment." In *Proceeding of Interface 84*. New York: McGraw-Hill (1984):79.

"Long-Distance Phoning: Time to Get Fickle." *Consumer Reports*. Mount Vernon, New York: Consumers Union 51(5) (1986):302.

Lynch, Clifford A. "Linked Systems Protocol: A Practical Perspective." In *Telecommunications Networks: Issues and Trends*. Jacob, M.E.L., ed. White Plains, New York: Knowledge Industry Publications, Inc. (1986):67.

Lynch, Clifford A. "The Operational Issues of Internetworking." In *Telecommunications Networks: Issues and Trends*. Jacob, M.E.L., ed. White Plains, New York: Knowledge Industry Publications, Inc. (1986):115.

Markus, Michael J. "Satellite Security: Legacy of 'Captain Midnight'." *Telecommunications*. Norwood, Massachusetts: Horizon House-Microwave 21(6) (1987):61.

Martin, Horst-Edgar. "ISDNs: The Network Solution of the Future." *Telecommunications*. Norwood, Massachusetts: Horizon House-Microwave 20(9) (1986):69.

Mason, Douglas C. "Review of Gateways." *Telecommunications*. Norwood, Massachusetts: Horizon House-Microwave 20(4) (1986):66.

Matthews, Joseph R. "Competition & Change: The 1983 Automated Library System Marketplace." *Library Journal*. New York: Bowker Magazine Group, Cahners Magazine Division 109(8) (1984):853.

McCallum, Sally H. "Linked Systems Project, Part 1: Authorities Implementation." *Library Hi Tech*. Ann Arbor, Michigan: Pierian Press 3(2)10 (1985):61.

McCallum, Sally H. "The Linked Systems Project: Implications for Library Automation and Networking." In *Advances in Library Automation and Networking*. Hewitt, Joe A., ed. Greenwich, Connecticut: JAI Press, Inc. 1 (1987):1.

McCarren, V. Louise, Chairman (Vermont Public Service Board). "Funding the Future of the Telecommunications Industry: Managing Technological Innovation to Satisfy Consumer Demands. Thoughts on a New Social Contract." Montpelier, Vermont; June, 1985 (rev. July, 1985); 11 pages. (Presented: Rensselaer Polytechnic Institute, Saratoga Springs, New York, June 3–5, 1985.)

McGill, Michael J. "Telecommunications Networks." In *Telecommunications Networks: Issues and Trends.* Jacob, M.E.L., ed. White Plains, New York: Knowledge Industry Publications, Inc. (1986):137.

Meadow, Charles T. "Networks and Distributed Information Services." *Journal of the American Society for Information Science.* New York, New York: John Wiley & Sons, Inc. 37(6) (1986):405.

Mier, Edwin E. "Comparing the Long-Distance Carriers." *Data Communications.* New York: McGraw-Hill, Inc. 15(9) (1986):90.

Mier, Edwin E. "What to Do (and Not to Do) With Inside Telephone Wiring." *Data Communications.* New York: McGraw-Hill, Inc. 14(10) (1985):185.

Miller, Nicholas P., and Young, W. Randolph. "Access Charge Strategies." *Telephony.* Chicago: Intertec Publishing 207(12) (1984):99.

Moir, Ian. "Network Management Protocols: A Growing User Concern." *Telecommunications.* Norwood, Massachusetts: Horizon House-Microwave 21(1) (1987):110.

Morgan, William A. "Spotlight on Fiber Optics." *Business Communications Review.* Hinsdale, Illinois: BCR Enterprises. 16(4) (1986):44.

Mosley, Scott W. "Low Bit-Rate Packet Voice Systems." *Telecommunications.* Norwood, Massachusetts: Horizon House-Microwave 20(9) (1986):93.

"NARUC, California, Virginia Challenge FCC Preemption of State Inside Wire Regulation." *Telecommunications Reports.* New York: Business Research Publications, Inc. 52(51/52) (1986):17.

"NARUC Task Force Study Finds That AOS Industry Not Ripe for Detariffing, Deregulation." *Telecommunications Reports.* New York: Business Research Publications, Inc. 54(26) (1988):22.

"New Jersey Advocates Wants 'Identa Call' Hearing." Tariff Actions. *State Telephone Regulation Report.* Alexandria, Virginia: Capitol Publications, Inc. 5(16) (1987):9.

"N.J. Okays Trial of Controversial Bell Caller-Identification Service." Major Regulatory Actions. *State Telephone Regulation Report.* Alexandria, Virginia: Capitol Publications, Inc. 5(18) (1987):10.

"Notes on the News." *Telecommunications Reports.* New York: Business Research Publications, Inc. 51(5) (1985):49.

"NTIA Proposes Deregulating Most AT&T, Local Special Access Services." *Telephone News.* Potomac, Maryland: Phillips Publishing, Inc. 8(30) (1987):3.

Orloff, Jerry. "Mobile Communication." In *Telecommunications for Management.* Meadow, Charles T. and Tedesco, Albert S., eds. New York: McGraw-Hill (1985):227.

"OSPA Letter Notes Impasse On Ways to 'Splash' Calls to AT&T When Requested by Customers." *Telecommunications Reports.* New York: Business Research Publications, Inc. 54(34) (1988):36.

Panofsky, Wolfgang K. H. and Phillips, Melba. *Classical Electricity and Magnetism.* 2d ed. Reading, Massachusetts: Addison-Wesley, 1962.

Pheelan, James J. "Signaling System 7." *Telecommunications.* Norwood, Massachusetts: Horizon House-Microwave 20(9) (1986):87.

Powers, Pam. "US Sprint to Sell Microwave Net." *Network World.* Framingham, Massachusetts: CW Publishing, Inc. 4(36) (1987):4.

Pyykkonen, Martin. "Centrex Now, ISDN Later." *Telecommunications*. Norwood, Massachusetts: Horizon House- Microwave 21(2) (1987):53.

Ralston, Anthony; Reilly, Edwin D., Jr.; eds. *Encyclopedia of Computer Science and Engineering*. New York: Van Nostrand Reinhold, 1983.

Rehse, Jeremiah K. "DTS: A Logical First/Last Mile Choice." *Telecommunications*. Norwood, Massachusetts: Horizon House-Microwave 20(10) (1986):65.

Rey, R.F., Technical ed. *Engineering and Operations in the Bell System*. 2nd. ed. Murray Hill, New Jersey: AT&T Bell Laboratories, 1984.

Roberts, Michael M. "The Need for a National Higher Education Computer Network." *EDUCOM Bulletin*. Princeton, New Jersey: EDUCOM 22(1) (1987):9.

Rockwell, Mark. "FCC Releases Price-Cap Regulation Proposal." Communications. *Management Information Systems Week*. New York: Fairchild Publications 9(20) (1988):20.

Rogalski, James E. "Evolution of Gigabit Lightwave Transmission Systems." *AT&T Technical Journal*. Short Hills, New Jersey: AT&T Bell Laboratories 66(3) (1987):32.

Rose, Marshall T. and Cass, Dwight E. "OSI Transport Services on Top of the TCP." *Computer Networks and ISDN Systems*. Amsterdam: Elsevier Science Publishers B.V. 12 (1987):159.

Rosenberg, Jerry M. *Dictionary of Computers, Data Processing, and Telecommunications*. New York: John Wiley, 1984.

Rosenberg, Jerry M. *Dictionary of Computers, Information Processing, and Telecommunications*. 2d ed. New York: John Wiley & Sons, 1987.

Rosner, Roy D. *Packet Switching: Tomorrow's Communications Today*. Belmont, California: Lifetime Learning Publications, Inc., 1982.

Rovnan, Dave. "Something Special: Signaling System 7." *Communications Week*. Manhasset, New York: CMP Publications, Inc. 157 (1987):46.

Rutkowski, A.M. "Beyond Fiber Optics versus Satellites." *Telecommunications*. Norwood, Massachusetts: Horizon House-Microwave 20(9) (1986):112.

Rutkowski, A.M. "Emerging Network Switching Technology and Applications." *Telecommunications*. Norwood, Massachusetts: Horizon House-Microwave 21(2) (1987):40.

Salwen, Howard [and others]. "An 80 MBIT/S Token Ring for High-Speed LAN Applications." In *Proceedings of Interface 85*. New York: McGraw-Hill (1985):15.

Sanferrare, Robert J. "Terrestrial Lightwave Systems." *AT&T Technical Journal*. Short Hills, New Jersey: AT&T Bell Laboratories 66(1) (1987):100.

Sazegari, Steven A. "Network Architects Plan Broadening of Future ISDN." *Data Communications*. New York: McGraw-Hill 16(8) (1987):129.

"Seeking Revocation of Large AOS Firms' Operating Authority, Consumer Groups Hold Court in Front of FCC;..." *Telecommunications Reports*. New York: Business Research Publications, Inc. 54(30) (1988):10.

Sergo, John R., Jr. "The Evolution of the All-Digital Network." *Telecommunications*. Norwood, Massachusetts: Horizon House-Microwave 21(8) (1987):52.

Shacham, Nachum and Tornow, Janet. "Packet Radio Networking." *Telecommunications*. Norwood, Massachusetts: Horizon House-Microwave 20(9) (1986):42.

Sherman, Arthur E. "Trends in Telecommunications Technology." *Journal of the American Society for Information Science*. New York, New York: John Wiley & Sons, Inc. 37(6) (1986):414.

Sobol, Harold. "Technology and Market Directions for Transmission Equipment and Systems." *Telecommunications*. Norwood, Massachusetts: Horizon House-Microwave 21(8) (1987):41.

Solomon, Charles. "Exploring the Problems of Internetworking." *Data Communications*. New York: McGraw-Hill, Inc. 14(7) (1985):177.

Soloman, Richard Jay and Anania, Loretta. "Is There a Role for Satellites in a Fiber World?" *Telecommunications*. Norwood, Massachusetts: Horizon House-Microwave 21(6) (1987):32.

Spangenberg, Scott and Cote, Raymond G.A. "Views on a Network Analyzer." *BYTE*. New York: McGraw-Hill 12(8) (1987):191.

Stallings, William. "The IEEE 802 Local Network Standards." *Telecommunications*. Norwood, Massachusetts: Horizon House-Microwave 20(3) (1986):40.

"Status of Major FCC Inquiries, Regulatory Developments." *Business Communications Review*. Hinsdale, Illinois: BCR Enterprises 18(1) (1988):48.

Stein, Lisa. "FCC Proposes Radio-Based LANs." *Telecommunications*. Norwood, Massachusetts: Horizon House-Microwave 20(7) (1986):30.

Sundarrajan, Raj. "Fiber Optics and Data Communications." *Telephony*. Chicago: Intertec Publishing 213(7) (1987):59.

Taylor, Steven C. "Why Fe?" *Telecommunications*. Norwood, Massachusetts: Horizon House-Microwave 19(9) (1985):56y.

"TDM Reduces Channels by a Factor of 4." *Telephone News*. Potomac, Maryland: Phillips Publishing, Inc. 8(39) (1987):2.

"Telemarketing." *State Telephone Regulation Report*. Alexandria, Virginia: Capitol Publications, Inc. 6(6) (1988):7.

"Telephone Management Systems and Software." In *Datapro Management of Telecommunications*. Delran, New Jersey: Datapro Research Corporation, Report No. MT60-210-101 (1988):101.

"Text of Inside Wire Reconsideration Order Outlines Areas of FCC Preemptive Authority." *Telecommunications Reports*. New York: Business Research Publications, Inc. 52(48) (1986):18.

The Communications Act of 1934. Stat. 48: 1064 (Ch.642).

"The Fundamentals of Fiber Optics Technology." In *Datapro Management of Data Communications*. Delran, New Jersey: Datapro Research Corporation, Report No. CS10-690-101 (1983):101.

"The Fundamentals of Transmission." In *Datapro Management of Data Communications*. Delran, New Jersey: Datapro Research Corporation, Report No. CS10-100-101 (1983):101.

"The Wiring Issue That Won't Go Away." Opinions. *Network World*. Framingham, Massachusetts: CW Publishing, Inc. 5(38) (1988):30.

Tibrewala, Rajen K. "Feasibility and Economics of Alternatives to Local Loop." *Telecommunications*. Norwood, Massachusetts: Horizon House-Microwave 19(9) (1985):69.

Toth, Victor J. "ANI and the Caller's Right to Anonymity." Washington Perspective. *Business Communications Review*. Hinsdale, Illinois: BCR Enterprises 18(5) (1988):75.

Toth, Victor J. "Coping with Access Charges on Data Information and Enhanced Services Providers." *Business Communications Review*. Hinsdale, Illinois: BCR Enterprises. 17(5) (1987):35.

Toth, Victor J. "Inside Wire—Untangling the Confusion." Washington Perspective. *Business Communications Review*. Hinsdale, Illinois: BCR Enterprises 18(2) (1988):61.

Toth, Victor J. "Louisiana v. the FCC: States' Victory with Complex Implications." *Business Communications Review*. Hinsdale, Illinois: BCR Enterprises. 16(5) (1986):31.

Toth, Victor J. "'Price Cap' Regulation What Is It and At What Price." Washington Perspective. *Business Communications Review*. Hinsdale, Illinois: BCR Enterprises 17(6) (1987):32.

Turtle, Howard. "The Open Systems Interconnection (OSI) Reference Model." In *Telecommunications Networks: Issues and Trends*. Jacob, M.E.L., ed. White Plains, New York: Knowledge Industry Publications, Inc. (1986):41.

United States, Department of Commerce, Bureau of Economic Analysis. *Survey of Current Business*. Washington, D.C.: Government Printing Office 67(7) (1987):121.

United States, Department of Commerce, National Telecommunications and Information Administration. *NTIA Regulatory Alternatives Report*. Washington, D.C.: NTIA Report No. 87-222 (1987):79.

United States, Federal Communications Commission, Common Carrier Bureau. *Amendments of Part 69 of the Commission's Rules Relating to Enhanced Service Providers*, Notice of Proposed Rule Making, CC Docket No. 87-215, FCC 87-208. Washington, D.C.: Federal Communications Commission, Common Carrier Bureau; June 10, 1987 (Released July 17, 1987).

United States, Federal Communications Commission, Common Carrier Bureau. *Bypass of the Public Switched Network*. Washington, D.C.: Common Carrier Bureau, Federal Communications Commission, 1984.

United States, Federal Communications Commission, Common Carrier Bureau. *MTS and WATS Market Structure*, Memorandum Opinion and Order, 97 FCC 2d 682, 1983.

United States. General Services Administration. National Archives and Records Service. Office of Federal Register. 47 **CFR** Part 15, Subpart J. Washington, D.C.: Government Printing Office, 1986.

United States. General Services Administration. National Archives and Records Service. Office of Federal Register. 47 **CFR** Part 68. Washington, D.C.: Government Printing Office, 1986.

United States, Office of the Federal Register, National Archives and Records Administration. *The United States Government Manual 1988/89*. Washington, D.C.: Government Printing Office, (June 1) 1988.

Van Essen, Judy. "AOS Companies: Fair Play is the Way to Operate." Perspective. *Communications Week*. Manhasset, New York: CMP Publications, Inc. 193 (1988):15.

Van Houweling, Douglas E. "The Information Network: Its Structure and Role in Higher Education." *Library Hi Tech*. Ann Arbor, Michigan: Pierian Press (18)5(2) (1987):7-17.

Wallace, Bob. "AT&T Studies New Services." *Network World*. Framingham, Massachusetts: CW Publishing, Inc. 4(36) (1987):1.

Wallechinsky, David and Wallace, Erving. *The People's Almanac*. Garden City, New York: Doubleday & Company, Inc., 1975.

Warr, Michael. "Toll Fraud Costs $500 Million A Year." News of the Week. *Telephony*. Chicago: Intertec Publishing 214(19) (1988):12.

Webster's New Collegiate Dictionary. Springfield, Massachusetts: G. & C. Merriam Co., 1977.

Whitaker, Douglas. "Using Cable Television for Library Data Transmission." *Library Hi Tech.* Ann Arbor, Michigan: Pierian Press 3(1)9 (1985):35.

White, Charles E. "A BETR Solution." *Telecommunications.* Norwood, Massachusetts: Horizon House-Microwave 21(2) (1987):37.

"Who's Your Operator?" Once Over. *Consumer Reports.* Mount Vernon, New York: Consumers Union 53(10) (1988):609.

"Wrangling With AOS." Public Policy. *Communications Week.* Manhasset, New York: CMP Publications, Inc. 192 (1988):14.

"You've Got a Friend in Pennsylvania." AT&T Monitor. *Communications Week.* Manhasset, New York: CMP Publications 159 (1987):8.

Zinn, Stephan [and others]. "OCLC's Intelligent Gateway Service: Online Information Access for Libraries." *Library Hi Tech.* Ann Arbor, Michigan: Pierian Press 4(3)15 (1986):35.

1984 Directory of Computer-Based Services. Vienna, Virginia: GTE Telenet Communication Corp., 1984.

"1988: The Year of Operator Services." In *Datapro Management of Telecommunications.* Delran, New Jersey: Datapro Research Corporation, Report No. MT10-830-101 (1988):101.

"There comes a time in the affairs of men when
you must take the bull by the tail and face the situation."
W. C. Fields [1879–1946]

Study Guide

Chapter 1

1. Give an example of a way in which telecommunications has had an impact upon the way information services are delivered to users. What impact has this had on the user? What impact has this had on providing organizations?

2. Discuss why it might be advantageous for an information system planner to have insight into likely future developments within the telecommunications infrastructure. How might this impact decisions related to system design?

Chapter 2

1. Give an example of how time might play an important role in planning an information system.

2. How have the needs and expectations of information system users changed over time. Has the system itself had an influence on these changing needs and expectations?

3. Why is it important to manage risks to the fullest extent possible when designing or acquiring an automated information system? Within the areas of user needs and expectations, system technology and design, and the telecommunications network environment, where can risk be more effectively managed?

4. The author discusses the areas of functionality, levels of performance, and costs associated with telecommunications networks, and concludes that cost is the least important of these elements. Do you agree? Discuss what you believe the author means by "best" cost.

Chapter 3

1. Discuss how the introduction of competition into a regulated monopoly environment could have both positive and negative effects. What impact might competition have on prices? How might competition affect the ability of a regulated enterprise to

generate cross subsidies? Why might competitors choose to enter only certain markets?

2. Discuss how the concept of a regulated monopoly might be fundamentally incompatible with the concept of a free market and fair competition. Should regulated monopolies be held to the standards established by antitrust legislation?

3. What are "structural separations" and why did the Federal Communications Commission feel such a mechanism was necessary to avoid cross subsidization of regulated and nonregulated services as a result of its CI-I investigation? Might it be possible to generate cross subsidies where separate subsidiaries exist? Can you give an example? (Hint: Consider sales personnel as a possible example.)

4. Give an example of how telecommunications and data processing technology have grown closer over time. (Hint: Consider how telephone switching is done.)

5. In terms of CI-II, what distinguished an "enhanced service" from a "basic service"?

6. What is an "access charge"? Why was it necessary to implement access charges after Divestiture?

7. What is an "enhanced service provider"? Discuss why these ESPs might be apprehensive about competing with nonregulated affiliates of regulated telephone companies? (Hint: Who controls the local telephone network necessary to access these services.)

8. Discuss how the rate-of-return regulatory mechanism might encourage a regulated telecommunications carrier to make questionable or excessive investments in facilities and equipment.

9. Explain how lengthening the period of time over which a piece of equipment is depreciated could lead to lower subscriber rates within the rate-of-return regulatory scheme. What impact might this have on new or improved services?

10. Why does the FCC get involved with the registration of computer equipment? Distinguish between the "Class A" and "Class B" designations.

11. In general terms, describe how "inside wire" is different from other wire used in the telephone network. Using inside wire as an example, do you have any observations regarding the effectiveness of current telecommunications regulatory and legal practices and procedures?

Chapter 4

1. What is "customer premises equipment (CPE)" and how does it differ from other equipment in the telephone network? Is CPE always owned by the subscriber?

2. Give an example of "terminal equipment" that is not related to computers or data transmission.

3. Describe how "access channels" are different from "long-haul" facilities. Is this a physical difference, a regulatory difference, or both?

4. How does a "tandem" switch differ from a PBX or a local central-office access switch? (Hint: What is being switched?)

5. Describe how "circuit switching" and "message switching" differ. How does "packet switching" differ from both of the above?

6. What is a local access and transport area (LATA)?

7. Discuss the difference between a local exchange carrier (LEC) and an interexchange carrier (IXC).

8. Discuss at least two differing characteristics or properties of digital and analog signals.

9. The author draws a somewhat subtle distinction between the concepts of "integration" and "consolidation" of telecommunications traffic on a transmission facility. Discuss this distinction.

10. Describe the difference between a "serial" and a "parallel" transmission facility or interface.

11. Describe at least two differences between an "asynchronous" and a "synchronous" transmission facility.

12. What is a "modem" and what does it do? Are modems used on digital transmission facilities? Why?

13. What is the difference between a "baud" and a "bit per second (bps)"? Can they have different numerical values on the same transmission line at any given point in time?

14. Give at least one significant reason why modern high-speed modem devices encode more than one bit in a "symbol" for transmission.

15. What single characteristic of satellite transmission channels most often makes them inferior to terrestrial transmission mechanisms for certain data transmission applications and for voice conversations? (Hint: Consider the total distances the various signals must travel.)

16. Using 186,000 miles per second as the speed of a radio signal, show that it takes about 1/8 second for a signal to travel from the ground to a communications satellite in "geosynchronous orbit." (Hint: The distance to the satellite is about 22,300 miles.)

17. Discuss several ways that "optical fibers" are superior to other transmission media.

18. Discuss at least two separate causes of signals being "distorted" or "smeared" while traveling over a transmission channel. What effect(s) might this have upon the information being relayed, or the amount of information that might be relayed within any given period of time?

19. Why is it important *not* to ground telecommunications cables or wires at both ends?

20. Discuss at least one significant problem that can be created when telecommunications cables are spliced together without appropriate matching of their "characteristic impedances."

21. Compare "amplification" of signals with "regeneration" of signals. What would you expect to happen to the "signal-to-noise ratio" during both of these processes?

22. What is "equalization" and why is this technique useful in telecommunications systems?

23. Explain the role of "echo cancellation" in both voice and data circuits.

24. What is "multiplexing" and how is it used? Describe three separate multiplexing techniques. Discuss these techniques from the point of view of maximizing the amount of useful information that can be transmitted over a given telecommunications channel.

Chapter 5

1. Discuss the distinctions between local area networks (LANs), metropolitan-area networks (MANs) and wide-area networks (WANs).

2. What is a value-added network (VAN)? VANs are often promoted as being more economical than other mechanisms for providing access to remote computer databases. How would you expect the economics to be affected as larger volumes of traffic are required between given locations? (Hint: Use your knowledge of how major database providers that both use VANs and have private networks utilize these facilities.)

3. What is a "virtual private network (VPN)"? How does a VPN differ from a "private network"?

4. Discuss briefly a "tandem" network and what distinguishes this type of network from other networks.

5. Describe several distinguishing characteristics of the "integrated services digital network (ISDN)." Give an example of how this evolving technology might affect delivery of information services in the future.

6. Discuss how "Centrex" and "CO-LANs" differ from PBXs and LANs.

7. Discuss the significance of the word "cellular" in "cellular radio" systems. Explain how these systems enable many more simultaneous communications to take place using a given number of radio-frequency channels.

8. Describe briefly a "packet-radio" system and how it might differ from a more common packet-switched network that uses point-to-point telecommunications channels between switching nodes. Can you give an example of how this technology might be used within a local information system? To access a national system?

9. What is a "very small aperture terminal (VSAT)" and why are they generally only used with large numbers of stations?

10. What is "local area data transport (LADT)"? How does LADT differ from some "packet data networks (PDNs)" that are now offered by some local telephone companies? (Hint: These PDNs often require modems to dial into the network using a local telephone line.) How do both LADTs and PDNs differ from VANs? (Hint: Consider service areas.)

11. Explain the difference between a "logical topology" and a "physical topology" within a telecommunications network. Can they be different within the same network?

12. What is "common channel signaling (CCS)" and how does this differ from the way signaling has historically been accomplished within the switched telephone network?

13. Describe the major difference between a "broadband" and a "baseband" local area network (LAN). How does this relate to time-division and frequency-division multiplexing techniques?

14. Explain the major difference between "carrier sense multiple access" and "token" techniques for arbitrating telecommunications channel use. How does this differ from "polling" techniques?

15. Give a simple explanation of what a telecommunications protocol is (i.e., in conceptual terms) and why such a concept is necessary.

16. Give an example of how protocol standards might contribute to more effective telecommunications implementations. Can you cite an example where this might *not* be the case?

17. Discuss several aspects of LANs and PBXs where, using current technology, each aspect would appear better suited for one or the other technology.

Chapter 6

1. Discuss how technology, economics, and politics all affect the telecommunications environment. Do you agree that it is impossible to separate these elements completely and isolate their various impacts? Can you give an example of why this might be the case?

2. Discuss how telecommunications and computer technology have grown closer together over time.

3. Give an example of how politics has had an influence on the telecommunications regulatory process. Was this a positive or negative influence?

4. Differentiate the roles of Congress, the FCC, the Executive, and the Judicial branches with regard to regulation of the national telecommunications industry. Can you give a recent example of conflict between these roles? (Hint: Examine the administration of the Modified Final Judgment.)

5. Under what circumstances does the federal government have jurisdiction over telecommunications? Can you cite an example where federal regulation would appear to exceed these criteria? (Hint: Examine the various criteria the FCC has used to assert "preemption.")

6. The Modified Final Judgement delineates between interLATA (i.e., between LATAs) and intraLATA (i.e., within a LATA) telecommunications traffic and what carriers are allowed to carry each type of traffic. Describe these restrictions. Can you explain why the court imposed these restrictions? (Hint: Consider the conflict between "monopoly" and "competition.")

7. Discuss the role of federal jurisdiction versus state jurisdiction with regard to interLATA traffic (see question 6).

8. Within a LATA certain elements of the local telephone network may be used for both intraLATA and interLATA traffic. Discuss the roles of both federal and state regulatory bodies with regard to these elements. (Hint: Consider "separations procedures.")

9. Frequently private network elements within a given state are acquired under terms of federal (i.e., *not* state) tariff. Discuss the concepts of "contamination" and "intent" with regard to this situation. There is a somewhat subtle distinction between contamination and intent. Can you explain the difference?

10. Describe the difference between "value-based pricing" and "cost-based pricing." How do these differ from "strategic pricing"? The Communications Act prohibits "discriminatory pricing." Does this appear to be at odds with the concept of "strategic pricing"? How?

11. Describe briefly what "bypass" is. Discuss how bypass has impacted the shift from value-based toward cost-based pricing.

12. Explain the difference between "special access" and "switched access" facilities.

13. What is "local measured service (LMS)"? How does this differ from "flat-rate service"? What impact might mandatory LMS have on the cost of access to remote databases using the switched telephone network?

14. Discuss how the procurement process within an organization might be impacted by deregulation and/or detariffing of telecommunications services. What constituted a legal contract for such services within the regulated and tariffed environment? Is the buyer protected in the same manner within a detariffed/deregulated environment?

Chapter 7

1. Discuss the distinction between local telephone company operator services and those offered by interexchange carriers. How do these differ? Describe how 0 and 00 are frequently used to access these various services.

2. Explain the difference between a "line-side" and "trunk-side" connection to a telecommunications switch.

3. What is "Feature Group Access"? Describe briefly FGA, FGB, FGC and FGD, and provide at least one distinguishing feature of each.

4. Discuss "presubscription." Is it possible to use a long-distance carrier to which a subscriber line is not presubscribed? If so, describe briefly how this might be accomplished.

5. Explain the difference between an "O-plus" and an "O-minus" operator-assisted call. What is a *bong-tone*?

6. What is an "alternative operator service (AOS)"? Can you give an example of a problem that might result from using such a service?

7. Describe what is meant by a "back-hauled" call. Why are these calls sometimes confusing with regard to billing?

8. What is a "splashed call"? Explain how splashed calls can result when calls are back hauled. How do splashed calls frequently appear on the telephone bill?

9. "Answer supervision" is a technique wherein it can be determined for billing purposes whether or not, and exactly when, a telephone call was completed. Do all telephone systems have this capability? If not, how is it determined for billing purposes when, or whether, a call was completed? What might be the effect(s) of such a method?

10. What is "automatic number identification (ANI)"? Give an example of how ANI can be used to provide a beneficial function within a telecommunications system. Can you give an example of how ANI might be misused?

11. Describe "station message detail recording (SMDR)" and how it is typically used within a telecommunications system.

12. What is an "auto-dialer"? Give an example of a problem that auto-dialers have caused.

13. Describe what is meant by "direct inward dialing (DID)." How does this differ from "direct outward dialing (DOD)"?

14. What is an 800 service?

Chapter 8

1. Discuss why there are many more private data networks than private voice networks currently in existence. How might this change in the future? Why?

2. The author claims that a five minute walk with a 360 KByte disk constitutes a 9600 bps communications channel. Support this contention by carrying out the necessary mathematical calculation. (Hint: Remember that there are 8 bits in each byte.) Can you verify that a 2400 foot reel of 1600 character-per-inch magnetic computer tape shipped by overnight express mail also constitutes a communications channel of about 9600 bps? (Hint: Assume overnight to mean 10 hours and 40 minutes — it makes the math come out even.) What can you conclude about the relative efficiencies and costs of online delivery of data records versus overnight shipment of magnetic tapes, when overnight delays are not a major factor.

3. Compare the various characteristics of a local area network (LAN) with those of a "data PBX (data circuit switch, or DCS)." Why might these differences be important when considering one or the other technology for a specific application?

4. Discuss possible advantages and disadvantages of public networking solutions (e.g., Centrex and/or CO-LANs) and private network solutions (e.g., PBXs and LANs) and what criteria might be considered when choosing one or the other for a specific application.

5. Speculate on the future of large mainframe implementations within the information services environment. (Hint: Consider the past and potential future evolution of distributed microcomputer technology and digital telecommunications facilities.) Is it the technology, the data itself, or the expertise and support resources of the supplier that is most important? How might your scenario impact the future structure of information provider organizations?

6. Discuss the role of "timing" when implementing and/or evolving information systems implementations.

"Everything should be made as simple as possible, but not simpler."
Albert Einstein [1879–1965]

Index

About the Author

The author currently holds the position of Director of Telecommunications Planning with OCLC Online Computer Library Center, Inc., where he has been employed since 1973. He has published numerous articles, and contributed to several books in the fields of Nuclear Physics and Accelerator Design, Computer and Information Science, and Telecommunications. He currently serves on the Editorial Board of *Library Hi Tech Journal* and is a contributing editor to *Library Hi Tech News*.

He is a founder of The Association of Telecommunications Professionals, where he currently serves as Vice President/President-Elect, and member of the Board of Directors. He has also served as a member of the Network Technical Architecture Group (NTAG) of the Library of Congress, and serves on the Linked Systems Project Technical Committee.

He holds a B.A. (1965) in Physics and Mathematics and an M.A. in Nuclear Physics (1967) from Western Michigan University, has worked for the Atomic Energy Commission at Argonne National Laboratory in Chicago, where he was involved in early computer networking experiments, and is a graduate of the Central States Universities-Argonne National Laboratories Honors Program in Physics, conducted under the auspices of the University of Chicago and the U.S. Atomic Energy Commission. He has held the position of Asst. Operations Engineer in the Cyclotron Department of Michigan State University, where he completed the course requirements for a Ph.D in Nuclear Instrumentation. He is a graduate of the Executive Education Program of the Harvard Graduate School of Business.

Colophon

This book was entirely produced using modern desktop publishing technology. The original work was done using the author's personal workstation, which consists of a *Leading Edge model D* personal computer with 640 Kbytes of RAM, a 20 Mbyte *MiniScribe* hard disk drive, a *Logitech C7* serial mouse, an *ATI 2400ETC* modem, and an *Everex EverTurbo/12* accelerator board. The 12-MHz, zero-wait state, 80286 processor, with its 8 KBytes of 55-nanosecond cache memory, which was added because the native 4.77 MHz 8088 processor was marginally adequate for a major project using desktop publishing techniques, provided an eightfold increase in effective processor speed. The 8088 processor is also retained for compatibility. Original copy was printed on a *Hewlett-Packard LaserJet* printer.

The manuscript was prepared using the *WordPerfect,* version 4.2, word-processing package. Design and layout were accomplished through *Ventura Publisher,* version 1.1, which was also used to generate the table of contents and the index automatically. The figures were prepared using *Logitech Publisher,* version 1.0. Final copy-editing and production were done using *WordPerfect,* version 5.0, and *Ventura Publisher,* version 2.0, respectively.

The camera-ready copy was produced on the *QMS-PS800* laser printer, using *Postscript* Helvetica and Times Roman software fonts in an oversized format with 12/14-point type for the body copy. Subsequently, the pages were photographically reduced to 84% of their original size to produce the final 10/12-point, 6-inch by 9-inch format. The book was printed on high-quality, low-acid-content paper to conform with the minimum requirements of the American National Standard for Information Science—Permanence of Paper for Printed Library Materials standard (ANSI Z.39.48-1984).